HOMESTAY
BASICS

Making Your Home Pay for Itself

ANNETTE SCOTT

BALBOA
PRESS

A DIVISION OF HAY HOUSE

Balboa Press books may be ordered through booksellers or by contacting:

Balboa Press
A Division of Hay House
1663 Liberty Drive
Bloomington, IN 47403
www.balboapress.co.uk
1 (877) 407-4847

Because of the dynamic nature of the Internet, any web addresses or links contained in this book may have changed since publication and may no longer be valid. The views expressed in this work are solely those of the author and do not necessarily reflect the views of the publisher, and the publisher hereby disclaims any responsibility for them.

The author of this book does not dispense medical advice or prescribe the use of any technique as a form of treatment for physical, emotional, or medical problems without the advice of a physician, either directly or indirectly. The intent of the author is only to offer information of a general nature to help you in your quest for emotional and spiritual well-being. In the event you use any of the information in this book for yourself, which is your constitutional right, the author and the publisher assume no responsibility for your actions.

Print information available on the last page.

ISBN: 978-1-9822-8031-4 (sc)
ISBN: 978-1-9822-8033-8 (hc)
ISBN: 978-1-9822-8032-1 (e)

Balboa Press rev. date: 02/14/2019

DEDICATIONS

This book is dedicated to Jo Bell and Michelle Sandford from Lewis School of English, whose help and support over the last few years have taught me so much.

I also couldn't have done this without the friendship of Vittoria Petronelli. My guest from Italy has allowed me to hone my hosting skills, practice vegan cooking and has forgiven me for my innumerable mistakes.

I would like to thank my family for tolerating my mood swings and for their never ending love and encouragement.

About the Author

This is a little bit about me and my journey.

I married early and had three children of which I am immensely proud. They in turn have given me thirteen grandchildren. I had a good corporate career with an international company. Then things changed quite quickly, I divorced and was made redundant.

So there I was a female divorcee of a certain age. One of the army of thousands of ladies who, in the late middle of my life found myself living alone in a family home that I could not pay for anymore. I became unable to work in a regular way due to family care commitments. The house was too big and empty.

It was the turning point where you feel your only option is to down size and become mortgage free. I didn't want to leave my home, of which I am very fond, and move into a one bedroom flat. That would have solved the mortgage problem but not the income.

So I set about thinking how I could earn some money using my home. I considered letting my home out for films but this was not going to be regular and as I don't live in London it was probably a nonstarter. I rented out a room to a lady for a while but it meant that I gave up control of part of my home and I didn't like it.

Then I saw an advertisement in a local paper for host families for a language school. A true light bulb moment, though at that point it was somewhat low wattage. It was a slow start and in the first year was only for the six weeks of the summer holidays and some odd weeks throughout the year. But I learnt a lot and found that some of the empty nest loneliness departed. I am not sure I would classify myself as an earth mother but I do enjoy having people to care for, especially as I was also getting paid.

That first year was a learning curve, I tried out different ideas and at the beginning of the second year, I agreed to host a lovely young lady from Japan who came through Lewis School of English in Southampton. She stayed for six months and it was a roaring success. She became a friend and six years later Saki and I are still in touch. She came to visit me over Christmas two years ago and I was thrilled to see her again.

During a previous incarnation, while I was married, I had worked for a multinational company and my office was based in Reading. My husband and I had a house in Hastings and I used to travel to the office several times a week. The distance each day was crippling and I was permanently tired. I tried to find somewhere to stayover on occasions to reduce some of the travelling but was mostly unsuccessful as hotels and bed and breakfasts were simply too expensive. I now realise that what I needed was homestay but it really didn't exist then. Or, if it did, then I didn't know about it.

Following a messy divorce and a very unwelcome redundancy, I went to Mongolia for a few months to work in a language school and an orphanage. The red wine session that began the process is a whole other story.

I was collected at the airport and taken to the family that was going to host me. The whole thing was one of the best experiences of my life. The host family were a grandmother and granddaughter in what we would term a one bedroom flat. They were so kind and welcoming but I was so far out of my depth that I was in danger of drowning.

One of the strangest things for me was that they don't have the concept of bedrooms. As a nomadic people, they live in round tents called Gers. In the city of Ulaanbaatar where I was staying there are both Gers and flats. Having a separate room for sleeping is a waste of space to them.

On my arrival I was shown into a room and told this would be where I was sleeping. It would have been a bedroom in a western flat but there was one glaring omission. No bed.

Mongolian people don't use beds. They lie down on the floor on something similar to a yoga mat. No sheets, pillows, blankets etc. I was stunned.

That time in Mongolia allowed me to experience first-hand how others feel when they come to my home. What we take for granted as normal in our country is not always normal in another. I have tried to use that to help others.

So, back to my lightbulb moments, I was coming to realise that I had to make my home pay for itself and maybe throwing myself into homestay was the way to do it.

Five years ago I decided to turn a small, secondary income into a slightly bigger main income. The wattage on the light bulb was increasing. I looked for books on how to run a homestay and couldn't find any. I found a few books on running bed and breakfasts and extracted anything that seemed relevant. Eventually I bought a book by Yvonne Halling called Bed and Breakfast Magic. I knew I didn't want to commit to bed and breakfast but hoped there may be some tips to help me. I was enthused by the book and found a lot of information that was useful. She was inspiring. Then and there my light bulb turned to a full beam spotlight.

After surfing the internet, I found a Homestay website that was offering to put homestay hosts in touch with homestay guests and I went for it.

As I live near to a university, most of my guests are young foreign students who stay from September until June and then I take language school students from June until September. I have up to four rooms occupied at any given time, though certainly not always with students. At the time of writing, I have a middle aged English gentleman who needs somewhere to stay for two nights as he is away from home working in another office. He is an exact match for my situation several years ago.

However you earn your living you will have to give up something of yourself in order to earn money. Working nine to five in an office is not for everyone and neither is running a homestay. But I have found a way that ticks most of the boxes for me. I have freedom for a good deal of my day and the flexibility to do as I please including writing this book. I have lost some of the privacy of my home as I share it with others, but I have gained such a lot. I can't imagine living in a largish home alone, with no-one to chat to or cook for. Going out to work each day and coming home to an empty house can be demoralising.

If I want to go on holiday, I have to plan in advance but is that really so different than if I was working in an office? I can't commit to the pressures of corporate life anymore but I can earn more by staying at home as a host than I would by going out to a minimum wage job.

For me it is the best decision I could have made.

My family lives locally so rarely need to come to stay but I do have lots of contact. My three children and thirteen grandchildren are highly supportive of my lifestyle choice and I am able to be around to help my family when I am needed. It's a win win situation.

CHAPTER 1

INTRODUCTION

Homestay has evolved into a very big business sector in a relatively few years. It is a new phenomenon. But actually, it's not. Travellers have been staying in other peoples' homes, tents, castles and caves for thousands of years.

When I was very young, my father was away at college and my mother took in three teachers from a local school as lodgers to help with the finances. One of these gentlemen became a lifelong friend and sadly died recently.

Taking in lodgers has been around for a very long time. They are people who live in your home, share some of your rooms but have their space. Some of you may remember relatives telling stories of people being billeted at their home during the war. This was homestay but was enforced by the government. Now we have choices. It is your home and a lodger does not have the right to exclude you from any part of it as a tenant would.

Whilst lodgers were not generally travellers, they were sometimes students, people working away from home for periods of time or people needing somewhere to stay whilst looking for permanent accommodation.

Legally there is no distinction between a lodger and a homestay guest. We have just learnt to formalise, update, repackage and advertise in a different way of late.

Homestay is about ordinary people living in an ordinary house welcoming others as guests into their home. The homeowner acts as a host and guide in return for a fee. This means that hosts can earn money by staying at home. It doesn't get much better than that!

Throughout this book I have included some small Value Added Tips (VAT). They are aimed at helping you highlight some important points that I have learnt over the last seven years.

The Difference Between a Bed and Breakfast, a Homestay and Rent a Room

- A bed and breakfast is a commercial enterprise that provides overnight accommodation and (usually) a cooked breakfast. Guests are expected to be out of the room during the day and to seek dinner elsewhere, though some do provide an evening meal for an extra price. Guests usually stay for a few nights only. They are a cheaper alternative to a hotel. It is unusual for a bed and breakfast not to have en-suite rooms these days. Some however, specialise in 'working men's' accommodation and are very basic. Others may have antiques and designer décor appealing to more discerning tourists. The owner's accommodation will be entirely separate from the guest areas.

- Homestay is a non-commercial, private home that provides warm friendly accommodation for a guest in someone else's home. It becomes the guest's home for the duration of the stay. A light breakfast is included. Whilst some expect guests to self-cater, many will provide an evening meal for an extra amount or included in the overall price. Guests can stay for a couple of days or up to a year.

  Homestays can be found anywhere but are typically in a residential area. They don't have Michelin stars, nor do they have AA stars or are part of accreditation schemes. They are relaxed family homes with shared bathrooms.

- Many people supplement their income by renting out a room. Indeed the government wants people to do this so they allow you to earn a certain amount every year tax free. Renting a room to someone means that the homeowner gives up a certain amount of control. They are not guests, they are tenants and have a contract with legal rights. They don't interact with the family and the owner does not provide food or any other service. They may or may not share a bathroom. Tenants will usually live an autonomous life.

What Will Homestay Do For You?

Homestay allows you to use your home to pay for itself and to have the flexibility to live a style of life that suits you. Some people will use homestay as a secondary source of income, some as their primary income giving up the rat-race entirely. Some hosts can earn more from homestay than in a full-time job.

Some hosts will choose to only have one guest at a time and others will have multiple guests. Some will be available 365 days a year, others for just a few weeks in the summer.

Homestay is about putting you in control and giving you lifestyle flexibility.

Why Do Guests Choose Homestay?

Most people choose a homestay over more traditional accommodation for two reasons, price and a homely atmosphere. Hotels can be impersonal, cheap bed and breakfasts can be drab as well as impersonal. Nice bed and breakfasts can be expensive and impersonal for a lengthy stay.

Homestay provides a good balance between comfortable and cheap.

The freedom of travel that we enjoy these days combined with the internet has made for a boom in overseas travellers looking for accommodation and being able to search and book from their own country.

There are many people who come as tourists; some come on work placements, others to find work and still more as students to study.

Some are young, frightened and homesick, others are brash and confident. All need help to a greater or lesser extent with living in a new country.

Foreign guests have another reason for choosing homestay. It will help them improve their English skills and learn about our culture in ways that other styles of accommodation cannot provide.

The family of a young, non-British person can also take a good deal of comfort from the idea that their child will be in a nurturing environment which is safe. Hotels and bed and breakfasts cannot offer this.

Not all guests are non-British. There are a great many British people travelling for similar reasons.

Whatever their origin they all need somewhere to stay.

Types Of Guests

There are many types of guests looking for Homestay accommodation. Here are a few.

- Foreign students away from home for the first time

- Students unable or unwilling to get Halls of Residence

- Students unable or unwilling to live in a shared student rental property

- People working away from home Monday to Friday

- People visiting friends and relatives who don't have space to accommodate them

- Guests attending a local wedding

- Actors taking part in a theatre production

- Visitors going away on holiday and need overnight accommodation before a plane or cruise

- Families of a student who are visiting them at college or university

- Sports fans attending a match or event

- Tourists visiting an area of special interest

- Business people away on a training course

- People completing an internship

- Medical staff on short term contracts

- Marriage breakdown persons needing a short stay for respite

I have hosted an example of each of the above. There really is no typical homestay guest.

I had assumed, as might you, that everyone attending a language school did so to learn English. Sadly, this is not always true. A very pleasant Russian lady who was a doctor came to stay with me for two weeks in order to attend a local language school. At least that was what her visa was for. It turned out that her daughter was at the university and she wanted to visit. Unable to get a tourist visa for some reason she got an education visa and spent the weeks shopping and sightseeing.

She obviously felt that the costs of the language school were outweighed by the cheaper homestay costs and the availability of the visa. I have no idea how prevalent this is. I have only encountered it once in seven years and the truth is it didn't affect me directly. She was a nice, respectable lady who bought me a very expensive duvet cover and pillow cases from John Lewis as a parting gift.

> VAT
>
> Not everyone is what they appear to be, but that doesn't necessarily make them a bad person.

The Five Secrets To A Successful Homestay

1. A personable host

2. A friendly atmosphere

3. Clean and comfortable rooms

4. A convenient location

5. A competitive price

There are several questions that you will be asking yourself by now. Such as:

- What do I need to do?

- How do I get guests?

- What should I charge?

- How much can I earn?

- What are the legal implications?

The purpose of this book is to answer these and many more question. By the end of the book, you will know if you want to begin and how to start. You will be comfortable with the process and have some ideas for the future.

Call To Action

- Identify the differences between a bed and breakfast, homestay and renting a room

- Recognise why guests choose homestay

- Decide what homestay could do for you

- Differentiate between the types of guests looking for homestay accommodation

- Examine the five secrets to a successful homestay

- Make a list of the questions that you need answering

CHAPTER 2

YOU AND YOUR EXPECTATIONS

Your Motivation

Ask yourself the most important question of all. "Why do I want to offer homestay accommodation?" There is no right or wrong answer. Some people are looking to give up a traditional job and are reassessing their priorities. Some want to earn a little extra to add to the family budget. Some have had a major change in their circumstances such as divorce, redundancy, serious illness, elderly parents, child care issues and so on.

If you have at least one spare bedroom then you can use your home to help pay for itself. It is, of course, possible to simply rent out a room but this gives tenant status and you will lose a certain amount of control.

Everyone has a different reason or reasons for wanting to run a homestay business. Here are a few.

- Earn extra money

- Work from home

- Run your own business

- Make your home pay for itself

- Not wanting to fully retire

- Want to leave the rat race

- Change of lifestyle

- Make new friends

- Company for you in your home

- Learn about other cultures

- Empty nest syndrome. The need to nurture but without some of the responsibilities

There are, of course, some cons when it comes to running a homestay. It doesn't suit everyone.

- Commitment to others

- Unless you plan ahead carefully you will be tied to your home for overnight stays

- No holiday pay, sick pay or pension unless you arrange it separately

- Loss of some privacy

- You can't spend the day in bed because you don't feel well

- A twenty-four hours a day, seven days a week job unless you plan ahead carefully

- Your income may be erratic

You and Your Family

If you are single then the decisions are all yours but then so is the responsibility. Having a family is a great help but a resident family is a two edged sword. If you have children living at home it can be a great experience for them. Living amongst other people sometimes from other cultures is a rewarding and educational experience. A partner who is committed to homestay is the best of all options while one who is not fully on board will probably lead to failure.

Family members and friends living outside your home will also have a part to play. They may be wonderfully supportive as mine are. But even they sometimes forget that homestay is my job. You have much more control of your life than with a traditional job but there are still some restrictions on your time and movements.

Some will consider that, as you are at home all day, you have lots of spare time and can come and go at will. The reality is you are running a business, which, although it allows you flexibility, does require your commitment. Dropping in for coffee will not always be a possibility.

Your Pets

It is important to consider any pets that you have. Are they friendly to others and will guests react well to your pets?

Even if you have caged animals including birds, you must make sure that potential guests are aware of their existence. There may be allergy issues, so the guest needs to aware of any animals.

Some cultures consider animals in a home to be unclean and your guest may feel uncomfortable.

Some guests may have a fear of a type of animal. You may be convinced that 'Rover' is docile but a large dog bounding up and barking is very unnerving for some. Me included!

I have a very even tempered and easy going cat called 'Precious'. Most guests take to her immediately but occasionally a guest is nervous.

Introduce your pet as a member of your family slowly and in a controlled way.

The very first long term guest I had was Saki from Japan. She was very nervous of Precious but was just beginning to feel comfortable around her. Precious is a very friendly cat and loves people.

One night, Saki got up for the toilet and didn't put the lights on as it is only three or four steps from her room.

Ablutions finished, she returned to her room and settled back into bed. I was asleep at the time in my room and was awoken by a blood curdling scream.

Expecting an attack by, at the very least, flesh eating zombies I did what every sensible person would do and rang the police. Oh wait, no I didn't. I ran to meet the attacker head on. After all, a middle aged, overweight 5'2" granny could certainly defeat the attacker.

Precious, taking the opportunity of Saki's absence had entered her room. Precious is a pure back cat and in the dark, poor Saki hadn't seen her. After Saki was in bed, Precious jumped on the bed to settle down to sleep. Saki, feeling the sudden pressure on the bed and seeing the glowing eyes thought all the devils from hell had attacked her.

I didn't need to defeat anything. As soon as the door was opened my poor cat ran for the hills and didn't return until the following day. Saki was eventually placated with a mug of hot chocolate and copious apologises.

> VAT
>
> Warn everyone if they don't want the pet in their room then they must keep the door shut.

What Should You Expect?

As a homestay host you will meet many different nationalities and cultures. Not all your guests will view the world in the same way that you do. If you are expecting otherwise then maybe hosting is not for you.

Cultural Differences

Most of these differences will be small to you but may be very difficult for your guest to come to terms with. Given time, patience and a lot of laughter it can all be overcome. Don't make changes to your life as they are with you to learn about the British culture. Just be you.

Your guests may not know what to expect and may be used to something very different. Culture shock is a very real experience.

It is up to you to be tolerant as guests often don't know that they are breaking cultural rules. You, of course, could also be breaking their rules.

Personal Space

Many cultures offer kisses on each cheek when greeting someone, even strangers. Generally, this is not the British way. On the other side, many Middle Eastern and Asian cultures do not welcome physical contact at all. I had a Japanese boy who stayed with me for a year. When he left, I gave him a hug goodbye. The poor man went rigid with shock. Unfortunately, I didn't learn my first lesson well. I recently had a Chinese man again for a year. He was very friendly and we had a good relationship. I instinctively hugged him goodbye. Same reaction. I had embarrassed him. Learn from my mistakes.

Another way the personal space issue manifests itself is in the size of the empty space we keep around us. A stranger who comes too close will make you feel very uncomfortable and want to retreat. Friends can get a bit closer before this happens. Your partner or child can come really close to you. In some countries, this circle of personal space is the same as ours, but in others, the circle is smaller. The result is we may become very offended because someone encroaches into our comfort zone, where in fact they are acting to their own cultural standards. You will probably have to live with this intrusion as it will be very much ingrained in your guest.

You can see this sometimes manifesting itself in queues. The lady behind you moves forward a little too far, so to relieve your discomfort you inch forward a little. Now the poor man in front of you is unnerved as you are too close to him so he moves forward too. Unfortunately, the lady behind you now feels they are too far away and so also moves forward. And so on. Claustrophobia and panic ensue. It is amusing to watch though.

Some cultures have a different view of personal space than others and some individuals have a different view of acceptable behaviour and good manners.

I had a middle aged Chinese lady staying with me for a few weeks as she was liaising with Southampton University. One day, I was cooking tea and she came home. I was boiling potatoes and hadn't put the lid on the saucepan. She marched up to my stove and placed the lid on the potatoes and then lectured me on wasting energy. My flabber was ghasted. I was speechless at the rudeness. Being a coward, I said nothing.

VAT

Moral of the story should be "stand up for yourself" or "give as good as you get". But in my case it was "you can't win them all".

Eating Food

British food is usually the biggest shock for foreign visitors. We consider our food and eating implements to be very normal, but then of course, so do they. Knives and forks can give people who usually eat with chop sticks a lot of difficulties. We tend to cut our food on our plate immediately prior to putting it on a fork and into our mouths. Many other cultures chop the food into bite sized pieces before it is even cooked. One pot cooking is also common. Be patient and give help.

Potatoes are a staple of the British diet but most other countries use rice. Don't change your habits but be aware of it as a potential issue.

Slurping liquid is very much frowned upon in British culture but is common in many others as is belching after a meal. It is good manners to belch and shows appreciation.

Explain to your guests that your food and cutlery is all part of our culture and that this is, after all, why they are staying with you.

Home Sickness

Some of your guests may develop homesickness to a greater or lesser degree. When they first arrive they will be excited and nervous, but this will wear off. Homesickness can develop in unexpected people so don't be surprised. Help your guest by providing security and a friendly face. Allow them to talk. They may retreat to their room and not want to socialise; preferring to sleep for long periods but as their confidence grows this will wear off.

Homesickness is an issue in its own right but is also a symptom of culture shock. Be kind.

Unusual Hours

This is a less common problem and for everyone's sake, you will need to head this off before it becomes a major issue.

Many nationalities have a different body clock from the British. These tend to be from hotter climates. They often eat later in the evening, stay in bed longer in the mornings and eat at different times of the day.

A young man from Spain arrived at my home at 10:30 one night. While he was unpacking, I closed down my house for the night. As I was locking the front door before I went to bed, he came down stairs and said he was going out. I was surprised but after all, it was up to him. I was awoken at 5:30 in the morning by said young man taking a shower and singing at the top of his voice. We had a few words about consideration for other people and I amended my house rules to say "no showers between 11pm and 7am". I also created a sign about being respectful of other guests. I was quite firm on this occasion and did not use humour as I would normally because other guests were disturbed by his inconsiderate behaviour.

VAT

Be firm and clear over your house rules.

Accents

No matter how technically good their language skills are, sometimes guests have an accent which is challenging. I am reminded of two separate guests, one a British man from Birmingham and the other a pleasant Chinese lady from Beijing whose English was grammatically very good. I really struggled to understand either of them. I had to listen intently and in both cases developed a headache if the conversation lasted for any length of time. Be patient, your listening skills may be tested.

Of course, the problem works the other way too. People may struggle to understand not only English but also your accent. You probably don't believe that you have an accent. You do. Try and slow your speech down a little and make your words clear. Don't overdo this however as you don't want to be condescending.

Call To Action

- Be clear on your motivation

- Understand and accept the downsides of homestay

- Communicate with your family so that they are aware of the issues you will face

- Evaluate the problems around your pet ownership for homestay guests

- Consider the potential for cultural differences and how you will feel about this

- Judge the effect of personal space issues on yourself and your family

- Recognise that homesickness has a debilitating effect on some guests

- Prepare to have difficulties with accents. How will you overcome this?

CHAPTER 3

YOU WILL BE A SERVICE PROVIDER

It is very much up to you how you want to run your homestay, as a business or as an occasional host. Neither is right or wrong, it depends very much on you and the area in which you live. I have written this book to assist you in setting up a successful business that will help you to have enough income to stay living in your own home, whether or not you have an alternative income.

Take from this the help and advice that you need and discard that which is irrelevant to you. It may also be that you start small as I did and then have a road to Damascus moment and decide to expand and take it seriously virtually overnight.

There are some serious questions that you will have to get to grips with as they will affect your decisions.

1. What makes a good host?

2. What type of people stay in Homestays?

3. What type of accommodation does your area need?

4. Why do people come to visit?

5. What services can you provide?

6. What are your limiting factors?

What Makes A Good Host?

I believe a good host is simply someone who has a genuine interest in other people; a people person. Hosts come in all shapes and sizes, singles, couples, employed, unemployed, working, retired, parents, empty nesters, the lonely looking for company and of course pet owners.

An outgoing nature, an organised mind and a good sense of humour will also help a great deal.

Homestay allows you to retain control of your home and is a perfect way to have people around you from other areas, cultures or religions.

Strong religious views may cause a problem for you with some guests. Obviously, you must not attempt to make a convert to your faith but you must be genuinely prepared to accept and respect others' views. For example, Muslims are required to pray five times a day and must face Mecca when they do this. They may need to rearrange the furniture in their room to allow them space for prayer.

Everyone in your home must fully understand what Homestay will mean for them and be in agreement. The support of your family is crucial. Although my children are grown up with families of their own, they know not to phone me between 6pm and 8:30pm. This is guest dinner preparation and eating time. I think of this in the same way as being at work. Personal calls during a work period should only happen in an emergency.

The secret of being a good host is organization.

If you have strong opinions or are a shy person who does not like their routine to be interrupted then maybe you should rethink this venture. If you prefer to sit at home alone reading a book and find other people an intrusion then Homestay hosting will not be for you. You will need to be able to make concessions. For me, the rewards outweigh the restrictions.

Everyone who becomes a host will have different reasons and hosting may not be the right decision for you.

The Types Of People Looking For Homestay Accommodation

There are really only three types of guests, but many fit into two out of three categories:

- **Those that want a cheap place to stay for a short time**

    o   Generally easy to please if the price is low

    o   Usually British or European

    o   Sometimes relocating starting a new job in the area but don't have anything permanent yet

    o   Usually a couple of days up to a couple of weeks. You will, therefore, have more changeovers and lower occupancy levels

- **Those that want to stay for a longer period but without the bother of renting their own place**

    o   Usually a little older working people

    o   Students who don't want to move into a student house or to cook and clean for themselves

    o   Business people who work away Monday to Friday and go home at the weekend

- **Those that want to improve their English and understand the culture**

    o   Usually young and nervous

- o   Usually not British but could be from any one of the hundreds of other countries

- o   Length of stay varies. Vittoria was an Italian student who came to me for her first year at university and stayed for five years

- o   Some will attend university, college or a language school

- o   Some will be tourists

- o   I had one really nice French gentleman who had taken early retirement due to ill health and came to me for six months. He volunteered in a charity shop three mornings a week and went to a language school every afternoon

Providing Accommodation For Multiple Guests

There are a number of things that will affect this.

- •   Do you have rooms and bed for multiple guests?

  - o   You cannot generally expect strangers to share a room. However, friends, couples or families may actually want to share on the assumption that it will be cheaper.

- •   Even if you have enough bedrooms, do you have enough bathrooms?

  - o   Whilst a family of five or six may be able to work around one bathroom that incorporates the only toilet, a group of paying guests will not.

- •   Are your guests all over eighteen?

  - o   It is very unwise to accept bookings for young people and adults at the same time unless they are related.

- Are your guests from a school or agency?

  o Check to find out their policy. Usually, schools will not allow guests using the same language to live together as they are expected to practice their language skills in your home. There are exceptions when the family of the guest has asked for friends or relatives to be accommodated together.

  o Language schools will not usually allow a mix of adults and children

  o They usually will not allow you to have both boys and girls under eighteen

  o They will control who they give you but will expect you to be careful if you are taking guests from other places

  o Language schools may require a Disclosure and Barring Service (DBS) certificate. This is a simple process that you can do on line. Its purpose is to prove that you have no criminal convictions in relation to working with vulnerable people

Type Of Accommodation Needed In Your Area

Your location usually dictates the type of people that will want to stay with you. Yes, it does matter, but you can have guests whatever your location.

- **University or college,** are you within walking distance or on your bus route? Particularly foreign students are always looking for somewhere to stay and unless they are allocated halls it is very difficult for them. Often families are very worried about their young person going to live abroad and are anxious. A homestay is a very good option as they feel their loved one will be safe.

- **Tourists** love city centres, country side and theme parks. They will attract tourists who want somewhere to stay.

- **Language schools** are always looking for host families. They are a good way for you to learn and hone your craft until you are ready to fly solo. It is how I started. Seven years later I still host for them in the summer months when the university students are less abundant.

- **Beaches** will always attract visitors and accommodation can be pricey. Bed and Breakfasts abound for a reason. I stayed in one in Blackpool once which was certainly illegal. My then husband and I and our three children all shared a room where there was literally no place to stand. It was a double sized room but contained a double bed, a set of bunk beds and two single beds. That was thirty years ago but I still shudder when I remember.

- **Football clubs** usually run academies where young up and coming footballers train so they need to provide accommodation. It is worth approaching them to go onto their homestay provider list.

- **Sporting events** such as Wimbledon, football stadiums, cricket etc. Always attract visitors from a distance. I recently had a young man from Birmingham travel down for the weekend to attend a football match at St Mary's stadium.

- **Cruise ports** are also a source of guests who want to travel down the day before sailing. I provide cruise parking on my drive so offering overnight accommodation as well is often welcome.

- **Golf courses** can generate business for you as people like to go on golfing holidays. It's a specialist market but if you live near a well-known course and are a golfing person yourself it is worth exploring the possibility. Some of the big golf courses run scholarship programmes for young people so they need to provide accommodation. It is worth approaching them to offer homestay accommodation.

- **Fishing** holidays are similar to golfing in that it is specialist clientele but is worth exploring if you are in the right location.

- **Moorlands, woods and lakes** often have an abundance of hikers looking for somewhere to stay.

- **Airports** are a good source of overnight guests. Although I live near Southampton airport, I have yet to have a guest who is flying. However, I have twice stayed near Gatwick before a holiday so I do know that guests want the service. I just don't go out to get this type of business as, personally, I don't like overnight stays.

- **Business people** have many different needs. Some work away Monday to Friday, some are on a training course, others are relocating and some are doing rotations or internships. I even had a sixteen year old doing a week's work experience at a yacht building yard a couple of years ago.

- **Hospital** staff members are sometimes in need of accommodation. Nurses doing agency work often go to different areas for a few weeks as do locum doctors. Doctors in training frequently do rotations in different hospitals.

Decide The Services You Are Able To Provide

The only thing that you absolutely must provide is a room with a bed in it and a window that opens. Obvious isn't it. However, I was asked if my room had a bed in it by a representative of a language school who was a little embarrassed to ask. When I laughed I was told that they had to ask because they have previously had a host who thought it was Ok to put a blow up lilo on the floor of their child's bedroom. This is taking staying as a guest in someone's home a step or three too far.

The service that you provide will not just be the physical items that you can supply. This business relies very heavily on the personality and skills of the host. You.

What do you know about that a guest would be interested in knowing? Do you like to share your skills with others? If you are an artist, maybe others would like to share your hobby. Maybe you could offer to arrange golfing or fishing trips. If you are knowledgeable about your local area you could offer guided tours.

The way I approached the issue was to create a guest avatar and then to think about what this guest would need in order to be comfortable in my home. He/she is between nineteen and thirty years old and studying at Southampton University. I have even given my avatar a name, Lee.

- Lee is not British

- Lee requires accommodation from mid-September to mid-June or mid-September

- Lee wants a quiet place to concentrate on studying

- Lee wants to be fed regularly without the bother of having to think about it or go looking

- Lee wants a clean and tidy room but doesn't want to waste time with regular cleaning

- Lee needs Wi-Fi

- Lee needs to be close to the university

So now I direct my marketing to Lee. I create services that are aimed at Lee, I create my menus for Lee and I shop for Lee.

Actually, I have a second Avatar called Sam. Sam is between fourteen and twenty years old and is a student at Lewis School of English. Sam attends school in his/her own country and visits the UK for around four weeks during the summer months to extend his/her knowledge of English. I don't need to advertise at Sam as I supply host services to the language school that set the conditions.

Lee is older and therefore more independent than Sam. Lee is a long stay guest and has a better command of English than Sam.

Lee and Sam are my regulars but I have had many, many different types of guests.

Spend some time thinking about who your target guests are. They may be students, families, couples, tourists, sports persons, actors, medical staff or business people. This will probably change over time but it will help you to focus initially.

As a host, you must be able to meet the needs of your guests in a friendly and knowledgeable way.

What Else Is Important?

- **Food**

  Homestay involves some degree of food but it doesn't mean you always have to cook. Note, however, that if you have under eighteens' you will almost certainly be expected to provide a hot meal every day.

  o It is generally expected that a light breakfast will be included. Your interpretation of a light breakfast is perfectly acceptable so long as your guests know what they will get before they arrive. Imagine how you would feel if you got out of bed and went down stairs expecting a full cooked English breakfast and you find a mini packet of corn flakes sitting in a bowl on the table with a note from your host saying "milk is in the fridge".

o   Lunch is up to you. Personally, I don't do it. It is too much of a commitment to have to be at home to prepare it. Language schools often expect you to provide a packed lunch so I decided to advertise that I would make packed lunches for my other guests for a fee. I charge £3.00 for a five piece lunch. Sandwich, fruit, crisps, chocolate biscuits and a bottle of water. This is cheaper than a "meal deal" from the local shops and puts the money in my pocket, not theirs.

o   For dinner, I prepare a free two course meal. Either soup and a main course or main course and a dessert. I serve dinner at seven every evening. I do this as it keeps me in control. I choose what we eat; a menu is way too much trouble. 7pm is a good time as it allows for late comers but also makes it easy for guests to go out for the evening after the meal.

o   Self-catering is not something that I favour but it is a personal choice. Guests will need to eat, so you must think really hard about how you want to deal with that. Self-catering means that guests will have full use of your kitchen, utensils, fridge, freezer and sink. They will take an indeterminate amount of time to prepare, cook, eat and wash up. They will also need storage space. If you only have one guest then you may decide this is a good option to free up your time. But if you have multiple guests it may cause you some problems.

o   You could place a kettle and mug, tea, coffee and sugar and fresh milk in each room but you will need to go into the guest room every day to wash the mugs, top up the kettle and leave fresh milk. This is more the route of a bed and breakfast. The simpler solution for me is to show the guest where everything is down stairs to enable them to make their own. After all, in a normal family home you don't have a kettle in the bedrooms do you?

o   I also have fresh fruit available all the time and as I love to bake, I have usually got cakes on a plate in the kitchen from which they can help themselves. Not at all necessary but I think of it as Value Added.

• **Safety**

Everyone wants to feel safe so make sure that there are smoke alarms in every room and that your front and back doors have a secure lock. I don't have locks on individual bedrooms but it is something you may want to consider.

• **A homely atmosphere**

This is something we all strive for but it is next to impossible to describe exactly what that phrase means. However, we all know it when we see it. A homely atmosphere is cosy, comfortable, attractive and unpretentious. Valuable antiques and works of art may make your guests feel nervous.

• **Local knowledge**

Because you live in the area you will have an abundance of local knowledge, from where to get the best coffee to the bus timetables. Your guests will want to know how to get themselves around the area, where to find a local church and the best place to buy souvenirs. Tourist attractions will be easy, it is your local knowledge that the guests really want. Where are the nice places to go for a walk, which is the best hairdresser in the area, is there a golf course? Spend a few minutes thinking about what facilities are around you. You may want to produce a leaflet with local hints and tips. You could also go to the nearest tourist information centre and get a variety of leaflets for your guest to look at.

- **A shoulder to cry on**

This doesn't happen that often but your nurturing skills may be called upon, especially for foreign students.

  o   Good old fashioned homesickness can be debilitating

  o   They may be in a foreign country, away from home for the first time and suffering from culture shock. Never mind the daunting prospect of starting university

  o   I had a very petite young girl from Thailand who was being bullied by a male student at the university

  o   Another girl's boyfriend broke up with her because she had come to the UK to study

  o   One girl had an elderly family member who died while she was away from home staying with me. She felt guilty that she could not go home to be with her family and was upset

- **Congratulations**

This is the other side of the coin. Something great happens and your guest will want someone to share it with. It is very depressing to have a great piece of news and no one to share it with. That feeling of elation needs to be broadcast. They walk in the front door bubbling with excitement. It is a great feeling to be able to share moments and give support when they get a really good mark in a test, an experiment went well, their sister had a baby or just simply a birthday.

I had one young man staying with me for three months and his wife was due to give birth two weeks after he got home. The baby was born early, the day before he flew home. No one knew whether to laugh or cry. It was a happy time but so annoying. I was privileged to share it with him and was so glad he was not alone in a hotel room at that special time.

If you have a long term guest, like my avatar, Lee, they will almost certainly have a birthday while staying with you. But even if a guest is staying for just two nights they could be celebrating. It may be their first time away from home on their birthday and it may trigger a bout of homesickness.

As a host, be kind, give a card, make a cake, cook a special meal and take photos. Make them feel cared for on their special day.

- **Quiet place to study**

Don't underestimate this. Many students don't want to live in noisy student accommodation or in halls. I always state that mine is not a party house.

- **A friend to help with local and cultural problems**

It is not just students that have problems. Many foreigners are concerned and don't understand local customs. I get asked often about why we do certain things or don't do them. Thanking the bus driver when you get off a bus is a favourite, as is queueing. After all, it is well known that "An Englishman, even if he is alone, forms an orderly queue of one." (George Mikes)

- **Parking**

It will depend on the type of guest you have whether they need parking facilities. Most foreigners don't have cars but some tourists will hire a car. Business people often do have a car. If you don't have specific allocated or off street parking it doesn't stop you running a homestay, you just need to make it clear in your advertisement.

If you have off street parking such as a drive consider how many cars you can accommodate. Easy street parking is the next best, but check if you are in a permit holder's only area. Some areas have very strict rules. Failing that, you could investigate if there is a public carpark in the area.

- **Wi-Fi**

Of all the facilities that a homestay must have, a bed is number one and Wi-Fi is number two. You will need the internet to run your business of course but your guests will definitely want access. Most will make Skype or similar calls to their family within minutes of arrival. Without access to the internet contacting families would be very expensive, with the internet it is free.

Some of the youngsters bring iPads with them and I often find them walking around my home with their iPads facing forward and mum and dad on the other end. They take their family on a virtual tour of where they are staying. I then have to spend a few moments saying hello and waving at them.

Two young Russian girls propped their iPads on the table at breakfast and ate with their family every morning. It helped the girls and their families.

- **Printer**

You will need a printer for printing your invoices for your guests and for the information sheets. Guests frequently want items such as boarding passes printed as well. A printer that scans and photocopies will be very useful too. I had imagined that university students would want to print often but in fact they don't. The university covers most of their needs.

- **House Keys**

Every guest should have their own front door key. Without it they will feel uncomfortable always having to knock on the door and you will have to sit up waiting if they go out for the evening. After all this is homestay. Within a family, adults have keys and come and go at will. Guests become members of your family for a limited time and need to be treated in that way.

Health And Safety

This is obviously a very important part of hosting. Not only your guest's safety but yours and your family's as well. Follow some basic rules and most things will go really well.

You and your family

Record information about your guest, such as a phone number, home address and date of birth. Photocopy their passport or ID where possible if they are not British. This should be destroyed when they leave.

Your guests

Put up an information sheet in the guest's room to let them know the evacuation procedure in case of emergency.

On the information sheet, give your guest the 999 emergency number. Not all countries use 999 and they may not realise that we do.

Don't leave any of your own medication in the bathroom where an unsuspecting guest may have access.

Ask the guest to keep personal belongings in their room to ensure that one guest does not use something belonging to another guest.

All in the household

To protect yourself from potential legal issues and the guest from potential medical problems, do not give any medication, even simple aspirin, to a guest. You will be responsible if they have an allergic reaction.

Keep a basic first aid kit close by.

You must fit a smoke detector in each guest bedroom and at least one down stairs outside the kitchen door.

Lock the doors whenever you leave your house and at night. You will know your area and be able to determine if the doors need to be locked during the day when you are at home.

If your guest wants to have a guest of their own, make sure that they ask you first. I ask these guests to leave by 11pm to respect the quiet nature of the home.

Use your judgement if an overnight guest is requested. I don't have a blanket rule as most of my guests are adults and should make their own decisions. However, if I feel an overnight guest will disturb other guests then I say no. My house, my rules!

Individual room keys are always a great subject for debate. I genuinely don't have any advice. Personally, I don't think they are necessary and in seven years have not had a problem. For me, homes don't have internal locks except on the bathroom. Locks are for renters or bed and breakfasts, not homes. However, I may be wrong. Others have said that you should have a key so that guests feel safer. I have asked various guests in my home and none have said they wanted one.

Arrival And Departure Times

There is no right and wrong over arrival and departure times. Each host that you speak to will have a different view. If your guest is from a language school or agency they may well set these. If your guest is arriving at 10am on a plane then it would be unreasonable to expect them to wait until 4pm to check in. My advice is to be flexible. It isn't usually a big problem unless you are trying to do a quick turnaround. In which case I ask the current guest to vacate their room but they can leave their luggage down stairs and are welcome to sit in the lounge or conservatory until they need to leave.

Departure may be a little easier to set. I usually say 11am departure unless by arrangement.

This will be up to you to decide when you are considering the type of guest your homestay is aimed at. British tourists and business people are easier to manage concerning timings as tourist tend to control their own destiny and business people tend to arrive in the evening and leave early in the morning anyway.

Students and foreign visitors on the other hand usually have very little control of times as they are at the mercy of airlines.

Consider Your Limiting Factors

These will be things that whilst you might like to do or provide you can't for reasons outside your control.

Think long and hard about what may stop you from being successful or may cause you a problem and try to find a way around it.

For example:

- You have no parking available but there is a public carpark around the corner.

- You have to start work at 7am and will not be able to supply breakfast. Lay the table the night before and show the guest how to make their own tea and toast.

- You have a large dog and some people don't like dogs. Make it clear in your advertisement that a dog is in residence. A guest who doesn't likes dogs won't book, but others who are dog lovers will be encouraged to book.

- You have an old boiler so hot water is limited. Consider a combi boiler as an investment but if that is impractical put a notice in the bathroom making guests aware of the limitations.

- You live in the country a long way from public transport. There are many people who would welcome a stay in the country away from city smog. Build up the positive aspects in your advertisement.

- You don't like cooking. Allow guests to self-cater.

For every problem there is a solution. Even major problems like only having one room to let can be overcome by building an extension or putting a log cabin in the garden. You must decide if the solution is one that you want to take. Some solutions are virtually free and some run to thousands. Only you can decide its worth.

Call To Action

- Identify what makes a good host

- Recognise the type of people who visit your area and may want to stay in a homestay

- Decide what services you are able to provide

- Assess whether you want to or are able to host multiple guests at a time

- Appraise your limiting factors?

- Decide if initially you want to host with a language school, advertise privately or a combination of both

- Create an ideal guest avatar to clarify your thoughts and ideas

- Choose the types of meals that you will serve

- List the Health and Safety issues that may be relevant to you

CHAPTER 4

YOUR PROPERTY

Now it is time to have a good look at your property. Begin by walking out into the street and looking back at the front of your house. Imagine you are seeing it for the first time.

Take Photos

Take a photo and imagine it on a web site being used to advertise your wonderful cosy homestay. Are you drawn to it?

Next walk into the house and start taking photos:

- The entrance hall

- Kitchen

- Lounge

- Dining room

- Bathroom

- Each room that you are going to let

- Garden

These eight or more photos are examples of what you will post to encourage guests to book.

If you can, print them out and place them all on a table. Examine them critically. If you can't print them view them on your electronic device making them as large as possible.

This is a really important part of the assessment process. Photos will help you to be more critical.

There will be some things that you will need to buy but probably not nearly as much as you think. It may be possible to move things around to different rooms to get a better overall look and feel.

Maintenance

Having taken your photos and had a good look around you will have begun to notice repairs that need to be done.

Examples:

- Stair carpet in need of repair or replacement. Apart from not looking too good you don't want a guest to trip up

- Dripping taps needing new washers

- Broken light bulbs

- Broken front door bell

- Wobbly chairs

- Broken brick step outside

- Damaged decking

- Broken windows

- Torn curtains

- Missing lampshade

- Torn or missing wall paper

- Missing door handle

- Missing bathroom lock

What Rooms Must Be Available to Guests?

Most of this is obvious but I will cover it anyway.

- **Bathroom**. If your home only has one bathroom you can still host guests. Two is obviously better. A downstairs cloak room is useful too.

    A shower is cheaper to run and quicker to use.

    Macerating toilets are not generally a good idea. Guests will not be as careful as you and if they go wrong a plumber will not repair they will only replace. It will cost several hundred pounds.

- **Sitting room**. It doesn't really matter if it is a lounge diner or a separate room but having somewhere for relaxing is necessary.

- **Dining room**. Sometimes kitchen diners are fitted with a breakfast bar. This is fine but you really should have a table too. It is less important if you only have one letting room or are not offering a food option. For me, having a meal around the table and discussing daily events is one of the important highlights of life in a homestay.

- **Letting Bedrooms**. Even if you only have one single room available to let you can still be a successful host. The more rooms that you have, the higher your income will be.

Decoration

Does the décor in each public room look good or is it shabby? Torn wall paper and scuffed paint will give a bad impression.

Your house does not need to be pristine. Warm, cosy and welcoming wins every time.

Check the bathroom. A carpet in the bathroom is not advisable. It is a perfect trap for bacteria. It really would be worth investing in vinyl flooring. It is cheap and easy to lay yourself.

Cleaning

Thoroughly clean everything concentrating on the bathrooms and kitchen. Use bleach on the tiling grout.

Wipe down doors and skirting.

If you don't have a vacuum cleaner you will need to get one.

Laundry

Long term guests will need to wash their clothes and you will also have extra sheets and towels. I used the washing machine I already had successfully for the first three years but when it gave up the ghost I bought a new one with a larger capacity. Ironically a month after buying the bigger machine I hired a laundry service.

For the last three years, I have been using the services of a wonderful lady who picks up my bed linen once a week and returns them all clean and ironed. I hate ironing.

- I have three of those wire clothes dryers that the guests and I use on the decking to dry our clothes.

- Clare is my laundry angel. I couldn't do without her. She collects dirty bed linen and drops it off clean and ironed. Worth every penny. I guess there are entrepreneurial women all over the country who do this. I would give up a lot before I give her up. It is worth checking out in your area for people advertising to do ironing or as Clare, the laundry too.

House Keys

Every guest should have their own front door key. I put the key on a key ring. If it is just a key, guests often lose them. Learn from my experience.

I ordered some really nice key rings from a Vistaprint. They are in the shape of a house with "Southampton Homestay" and the phone number. They are really pretty and sensible. Individually not too much but multiplied by eight it came to quite a bit.

I waited for them to be delivered and was really excited (sad aren't I) when they arrived. I gave them to my guests and they swapped their keys onto them happily.

Then someone said "the phone number doesn't look right". I checked and sure enough, two of the digits were transposed.

VAT

Only one word, Proofread.

On one occasion, a young lady lost hers on a train when out for the day. I got a call from a gentleman at the railway's office. They kindly put it on a train back to Southampton and I picked it up. Having the phone number on the key ring paid off in that instance and has the added advantage of giving the guests an easy reminder of your number when they are out and about.

You may want to invest in a key safe. I find that sometimes guests lose their keys or leave them in their room when they go out. I put a key in the key safe attached to the wall outside my front door. If guests find themselves locked out they can phone or text and I give them the code so that they can let themselves in. The code is also on their information sheet.

Keys can be expensive. Always get them back from your guests.

Fire and CO2 Detectors

Each room that you let to a guest MUST have a smoke alarm.

You must also have a smoke alarm down stairs close to the kitchen but not in it as it will go off constantly when you are cooking.

Place a fire blanket on the wall of your kitchen.

You should also place a CO2 detector in the vicinity of your boiler.

Regularly change all the batteries.

Owner vs Renter

I am an owner so I give myself permission to take guests. If you are a renter, you may need to get permission from the landlord. Be very clear when asking that the landlord understands you are not subletting. The landlord's concern will be that your guests may claim residency and refuse to leave. The landlord would then be faced with legal costs.

Homestay provides guests with a licence to occupy not a tenancy agreement.

Check your tenancy agreement; it will probably say no one can stay for more than twenty-eight days. If so, you do not need permission unless you want to take long term guests. Language school, college or university students are also usually acceptable as they pose no long term threat to the landlord. If in doubt seek legal advice.

If it is possible, get permission in writing to avoid disputes in the future.

Call To Action

- Take before photographs to assist you in looking at your home dispassionately

- Identify areas of your home that may need repairs or updating

- Undertake a thorough cleaning

- Purchase extra door keys and attach a suitable key ring to each

- Evaluate your fire protection equipment

CHAPTER 5

GUEST ROOMS

Room Identification

If you have more than one room that you let out to guests you will need to have a way to differentiate them. There is something very cold and clinical about using a number. I have four rooms and I chose to name them: The Britain Room, the Beach Room, the Butterfly Room and the London Room. I bought a mirrored sign on Amazon for each room as an identifier for the outside of each door. The Britain Room has a map of Britain, the Beach Room has an Anchor, the Butterfly Room has a butterfly and the London Room has a Bucking Palace guard standing to attention. I bought a bath picture for the bathroom and a shoe for my own room.

None of my bedrooms have locks. I have thought long and hard about this and have polled my guests. Without exception, everyone I asked said locks were not necessary. The feeling was that homes don't have locks. To add locks depersonalised my home. In the seven years I have taken guests, there has never been an issue. Of course it only takes one time but currently, I don't want to go down that route. You may, however, feel differently.

Facilities

Each room that you let will need to have certain items, some are essential and some are really nice to have to add value and comfort for your guest. However, a working window is a must have.

Guests will spend a great deal of their time in their room and if they are staying for up to a year this will amount to a great many hours.

Essentials

A window: this must open fully and should be lockable.

Curtains or blinds: pretty and clean window covering will make the room feel warm and cared for. They may need to have blackout linings if you are in a well-lit area at night.

Two double sockets: one at each end of the room.

A bed: obvious I know, but I have heard tales of children from language schools being expected to sleep on a mattress on the floor. It should have a headboard but no baseboard. This is because some guests come in XXL. My grandson, Dane is 6'8" and the length of a bed is always problematic for him.

A bedside table: I use sets of drawers in the single rooms so that I can save space. You should have a bedside light on the table too. I have stayed in places where I have had to get out of bed to switch off the light then fumble my way back in the dark.

Wardrobe: give plenty of hanging space. My wardrobes have all got hanging and integral drawers.

Coat hangers: do not use wire hangers from the dry cleaners! They look cheap and can damage clothes. I like the flocked or wooden ones from IKEA. Garments don't slip off them.

Desk and chair and lamp: most of my guests are students and need study space. If you are on a budget, Ikea does a range of tables with screw on legs that means you can include a desk in your guest rooms for about £15. Make sure the chair is reasonably comfortable as they may spend many hours at it. If your guest is not a student, the desk easily doubles as a dressing table. A desk lamp is also necessary. Make sure the desk is placed near one of the double sockets so that computers etc. can be plugged in.

Full length mirror: place it near an electric socket so that your guest can dry their hair easily.

Waste bin: I always line my bins so that we can tie off and empty the bins easily.

Laundry basket: I always provide my guests with one of those collapsible baskets. They are cheap and mean that the guests who are staying for longer time periods don't have to look at a pile of dirty washing on the floor. They can easily take it down stairs to use my washing machine.

Hair dryer: Many of my guests arrive on a plane and hair dryers are heavy. They also often have the wrong plug type. Hair dryers are cheap and guests like to know they are available. Make sure to state in your room description that you they are available.

Fire alarm: Every guest room MUST have a working smoke alarm with new batteries.

Evacuation procedure: You MUST display instructions so that your guest knows what to do in the event of a fire. You can see an example in the appendix.

Information sheet: I have a sheet of A4 printed with various pieces of information that the guest may need to know, such as Wi-Fi and password, dinner times, basic house rules etc.

Towels and bedding

Mattress protector: It is essential that you use protectors. The repercussions could be very expensive. Stained mattresses are not acceptable to guests and I am afraid they can be subject to assault by bodily fluids, hot drinks and spilt cans or bottles.

Pillows: each bed should have two or four pillows. I don't use pillow protectors as I prefer to regularly replace pillows anyway. If you can have extra pillows available as many people prefer to have three or to use a third to prop themselves up when sitting in bed.

Duvet: personally I prefer duvets but many people swear by blankets. I have tried washing duvets but generally, it is not worth it. They are cheap to buy so I replace regularly.

Duvet covers and pillow cases: always use matching sets. You will need to have at least three sets per bed; one on the bed, one in the linen cupboard and one in the laundry. My rooms are themed so the linen matches the theme. Obviously, this is your choice.

Fitted sheets: this is an age old debate. Flat sheet versus fitted. Personally, I prefer fitted as they don't move about on the bed so much and always look tidy. However, they don't iron very well and are more difficult to store.

Towels: again you will need three sets per bed. I fold a bath sheet, bath towel and a face flannel into a tower and place them on the freshly made bed.

Extra Touches

All of the following are added extras. They are really good touches to make your guests more comfortable, but if you don't have them you can still give a guest a good experience.

Alarm clock: most of my guests tend to use their phones as alarms these days, as indeed do I. However, they are cheap and small so you may want to consider them. I use the coloured cubes from IKEA.

Arm Chair: if you have space in your guest room, an arm chair is a lovely addition. Guests can sit and reflect, read and relax.

Cushions: cushions on the bed give a lovely luxurious feel to a room. A cushion on the desk chair and on an arm chair all contribute to a feeling of extra comfort.

Throw: a throw on the end of the bed also adds a luxury feeling and is a practical extra cover if it gets a bit chilly. A spare blanket is also a useful extra.

TV: I used to put TVs in every room but soon learned that students don't want them. They take up space and providing you have Wi-Fi, guests use their phones or iPads instead. I have a TV on standby if anyone wants it but it is more than a year since anyone asked for it.

USB port: I recently changed one socket in each room to have a socket with a built in USB port. I also have one in the Kitchen. If you haven't seen them then I would go and have a look. Each double socket with two USB ports only costs around £8, but then you need to get an electrician to fit it. I did it because I was constantly being asked how a guest could charge their phone. Brits don't have a problem but foreign guests have problems as their plugs don't fit ours. I still keep a couple of converter plugs but don't get asked so often anymore.

Dressing gown: an expensive addition but adds a sense of luxury. I had them when I started out but some went AWOL, some got stained and others were torn. I decided it wasn't worth the effort, cost and different sizes. It is worth thinking about, however. I bought them from Studio with Southampton Homestay embroidered free.

Toiletries: lovely to give away but definitely not necessary. I am thinking of trialling items for sale. Guests often forget things like toothpaste, toothbrush, soap, shampoo, shower gel, razor and deodorant. It wouldn't really be a viable income stream but would definitely be a great customer service.

Cleaning

I clean the rooms in two different ways, on exit and weekly during the stay. I aim to be as unobtrusive to guests as possible during their stay but the rooms still need to be cleaned. Most of my guests are out all day but some study at home. I always tell the guest that their room will be cleaned the following day. It gives them a chance to remove private items from view. I have a golden rule: never open a cupboard or drawer in a guest room. A feeling of privacy is really important. The guest must trust you.

Occasionally a guest may say they don't want their room cleaned. Whilst it is important to respect their wishes you will need to make a judgement call. I did have a young man who did not want his room cleaned during the whole year of his stay. Naively I acquiesced. When he finally left I needed to replace the carpet and treat and redecorate the whole room.

VAT

It is your home and you need to be aware of maintenance issues especially condensation problems when guests don't open windows.

Weekly room clean

This should take around twenty to thirty minutes

- Fresh sheet, duvet cover, pillow cases and towels

- Empty the bin

- Open the windows

- Check and replace light bulbs

- Check and replace smoke alarm batteries

- Sweep the floor

- Wipe all surfaces

- Wipe window sills

- Wipe doors

- A quick wipe of exposed skirting

On exit room clean

This should take around thirty to sixty minutes. Obviously, the extent of the deep clean will depend on the length of the previous stay. As many of my guests stay for the academic year, I deep clean over the summer.

I always make sure the room is cleaned and ready after a guest leaves as sometimes I only get a few hours' notice that someone will be arriving. It's best to be prepared.

- Fresh sheet, duvet cover, pillow cases and towels

- Empty the bin.

- Open the windows

- Check and replace light bulbs

- Check and replace smoke alarm batteries

- Sweep the floor

- Wipe all surfaces

- Wipe skirting

- Wipe window sills

- Wipe doors

- Clean windows

- Move the bed and clean underneath

- Check pillows and duvet. Discard and replace as necessary

Call To Action

- Decide how you will identify your rooms if you have more than one

- Evaluate each room and make a list of any items that you do not yet have

- Formulate a room cleaning plan

Chapter 6

BUSINESS PLANNING

You have looked at your home in detail, considered the area in which you live, contemplated your own strengths and are now ready to begin planning the business itself.

The first question you are bound to be thinking is "How much can I charge guests?" That will then lead to "How much can I earn?" You can also look at it the other way around. What do I need to earn? That will then dictate how much you need to charge. It is always a fine balance between what you need, what your expenses are and what the local area can take.

This will be your business and you will be the business. It's a two edged sword. If you are ill, what will happen? If you want to take a holiday you will have no income. If you have long stay guests you will need to plan holidays for when they have left. But the bottom line is simple: Your home, your business and your rules!

Having a holiday can be tricky when you have a high occupancy rate. Last year I was suffering a bit and really needed a break. However, I had three female Masters students so wouldn't be able to get away. Masters students stay throughout the summer, leaving in September. The next year's students arrive at the same time as the Masters students' leave.

Then I had a brilliant idea. I do sometimes. What if I took them with me? The Sun £9.50 holidays were advertising and you have to pay for four even if only one of you go.

I suggested to the girls that we all went for a caravan holiday in Devon. They could take their lap tops and books if they wanted to and as lectures had finished they thought it was a good idea.

We had a great week. Simple food, takeaways, beach and country walks, games of cards and DVDs.

So much to my family's amusement, I took my work on holiday with me.

VAT

Every problem has a solution

What Do Others In The Area Charge?

Do some market research or due diligence. Look at what local bed and breakfasts charge, budget hotels and student accommodation. If there are other homestays in your area, check them out too. Remember to compare like for like. Make a table to compare. A small table, even drawn on the back of an envelope will help.

Name	Type	nightly	Weekly	Breakfast included
The Grange	Hotel	£45	£315	No
Ambleside	Bed and Breakfasts	£30	£250	Yes Cooked
Gateway	Student Halls	XX	175	No
Mrs. Jones	Homestay	25	175	Yes light

With this information, you will be able to see what a reasonable price for the area is and what you are prepared to offer.

Remember that you are already offering more than the hotel and almost certainly the bed and breakfast and definitely the halls as you are providing a home with laundry facilities, regular cleaning, a warm smile and a shoulder to cry on. None of the others come close to providing what you can yet they charge considerably more. Of course, they will probably have bigger rooms with en-suite facilities but that is guest preference and there is generally nothing you can do about that.

Next, you need to consider what you can offer that the others in the area don't. This is your Unique Selling Point (USP). In my case, I offer a free evening meal. Of course, it isn't really free it is built into the price but everyone likes to get something for nothing. Also by offering a 'free meal', I head off the issue of guests who try to haggle for a lower price because they don't want to eat. I budget for £2.50 for dinner and that would be too small a reduction to make a difference to a guest's decision whether to book but a free two course meal is a big incentive for most people. My deal is, I cook you eat. If you don't want to do that it is perfectly fine and is your prerogative. My house, my rules!

What Will Your Expenses Be?

Now is the time to consider how much it will cost you to have a guest in your home. Be absolutely honest with yourself here. Look at your current water, gas and electricity bill. Remember that a proportion of your bill is standing charges so will apply no matter how many people are in the house. Divide the remaining monthly bill by thirty to get a daily rate. If there are two of you in the house then divide it by two to get the amount per person per night. Remember you are trying to find out approximately how much an extra body using up services will cost you.

Service	Cost for one	
Gas	£0.50	

Electric	£0.75	
Water	£0.75	

Now think about food. How much does a cup of tea or coffee cost? Assume a guest will drink three cups a day. What breakfast will you supply and how much will it cost? Dinner and snack costs also need to be added.

Service	Cost for one	
Gas	£0.50	
Electric	£0.75	
Water	£0.75	
Drinks	£0.15	
Fresh fruit	£0.20	
Breakfast	£0.95	
Soup and bread or dessert	£0.75	
Meat or fish	£1.25	
Potatoes/rice pasta	£0.20	
Vegetables	£0.20	
Sauces	£0.10	

Lastly, add in the extra cleaning services such as the use of the washing machine and change of bedclothes and towels. I change bedding once a week. You may want to change more frequently. Hotels, for example, change daily. I do my costings as if the guest is only staying for one night and then if they book for longer I can offer a different weekly rate.

Service	Cost for one	
Gas	£0.50	
Electric	£0.75	
Water	£0.75	
Drinks	£0.15	
Fresh fruit	£0.20	
Breakfast	£0.95	
Soup and bread or dessert	£0.75	
Meat or fish	£1.25	
Potatoes/rice pasta	£0.20	
Vegetables	£0.20	
Sauces	£0.10	
Guest washing powders	£0.20	Short term guest don't usually need to use your washing machine
Extra cleaning materials	£0.30	

Laundry of bedding	£4.00	This is only the daily charge for overnight stays. Longer term stays are much cheaper.

So now you know roughly how much an overnight guest will cost you by adding together all these amounts. In this example, a guest costs £10.30 a night. You will probably have different figures and may need to add in other expenses.

What Should You Charge?

There are lots of opinions on this and it all comes down to your choice. People do business Sales and Marketing degrees on this subject. It depends on how much you want to earn, what the local competition is and what the local call for your service is. What I charge in Southampton will be different from an almost identical set up in London or Cornwall. If you start with "I need to get £100 a night", you may get one or two takers in a year but not many people will stay with you. If you start with a rock bottom price, say £15 a night some will be suspicious as it is too cheap but many more will come and stay and you will be almost permanently full, rushed off your feet and exhausted with a very low profit margin.

I am sorry; I can't give you a magic formula. Suck it and see as they say. However, if you join up with a language school or a college they will set the rate. It is then up to you to accept that rate or look elsewhere. However, approaching one of these establishments and seeing what they are paying is a good starting point. Most language schools will pay less than you can get from private guests.

If you are going to advertise through one of the websites such as AirBnB or Homestay.com, they will charge a 15% booking fee so you will need to add that into your calculations.

Security Deposit

Consider whether you want to hold a security deposit. This would be payable on arrival and returnable when the guest leaves. Personally, I do not as it feels impersonal. However I admit that there have been a couple of occasions when I have wished that I did.

Holding Fees

A guest who is staying with you for a long time may need to go home or on holiday for a week or two. You can deal with this in one of three ways. Whatever decision you make it must be very clearly stated at the time the guest makes the booking. If your guest is from a language school then they will have a policy that you will be required to honour.

1. The guest retains the room, leaves their belongings in the room, returns at the prearranged date. The room is unavailable for you to rent out to others so you apply the full room rate.

2. The guest retains the room, leaves their belongings in the room, returns at the prearranged date. The room is unavailable for you to rent out to others but you allow a partial discount as they will not be consuming your utilities or food.

3. The guest goes away and takes all of their belongings with them. They move out and then move back in again at a later date. The room is then available for renting to others in the interim period.

Use your discretion. You will need to be flexible. For example, I allow university students to store their belonging in my loft when they go home for Christmas and Easter so they don't have to take unnecessary items on a plane. I don't charge for this.

Occupancy Levels

- **What is occupancy?**

    Your occupancy level will help you to decide what to charge and after you have been running for a while it will help you see more clearly how profitable your business is and if you should make some changes. It is only a guide.

- **Why does occupancy matter?**

    If all of your rooms were to be occupied every single night then you would have 100% occupancy. This would be the holy grail of the accommodation industry. Most bed and breakfasts have around 25%-40% occupancy. Hotels usually aim for 50%. I haven't fallen below 85% in the last five years. Your occupancy level is a guide to your profitability. Empty rooms mean lost revenue. Your occupancy level is the ratio of rented rooms to the total amount of available space.

- **Working out occupancy levels?**

    Begin with availability. Multiply the numbers of rooms that you are able to let to guests by how many days of the year you are willing to work. It is very common to make yourself unavailable over the Christmas period and for a couple of weeks in the summer. However, be careful to be available during the area's busiest time. In the case of university students, if I decided to have a holiday over the last two weeks of September my business would go under very quickly.

    In my case, I am open 365 days a year and I have four rooms so my availability is:

    $$365 \times 4 = 1460 \text{ nights available}$$

    This means that I have 1460 nights available in a given year.

After your business has been running for a few weeks or months you can check your actual figures against that which was possible. You simply add up how many rooms have been occupied in the previous period of time and compare the actual with the available.

Let's work an example: You have been in business for three months (ninety days) and have two rooms. Your maximum occupancy would be:

$$90 \times 2 = 180 \text{ nights available}$$

To determine occupancy rate begin by adding up the number of nights that the rooms have had someone in them. Let's say sixty nights. The formula is Actual divided by Potential multiplied by 100. So:

$$60 \div 180 \times 100 = 33\% \text{ occupancy rate}$$

Your occupancy rate for the three month period has been 33%. Just one extra night a week over thirteen weeks would mean:

$$73 \div 180 \times 100 = 40.5\%$$

Your occupancy level shoots up to 40.5%.

Another use of the occupancy level is to forecast income. The best case scenario would be 100% occupancy. If the nightly rate you are charging is £25 and your expenses are £10 then the maximum you could earn in this period is:

$$180 \times (£25-£10) = £2700 \text{ maximum}$$

A 33% occupancy rate reduces the potential of £2700 over three months to:

$$60 \times (£25\text{-}10) = £900$$

Set Up A Diary

A really good diary system is essential. I can't stress this enough. Set it up ready before you open your doors for the first time. I use a spread sheet but a one day to a page paper diary will be Ok to start with. I discuss the diary in more detail in a later chapter.

Month	Day	Date	Event	Room 1	Room 2	Room 3	Room 4
May	Tuesday	1st					
May	Wednesday	2nd					
May	Thursday	3rd					
May	Friday	4th					
May	Saturday	5th					
May	Sunday	6th					

Create An Information Sheet

An information sheet in each guest room is essential. You can put anything on it that you think is appropriate. A copy of mine is in the appendix

Do The Cleaning

Having decided that you are going to really make a go of homestay and walked through your home taking pictures, you will have a clear idea of where you need to put in some effort. Clean everything that a guest will come across. First impressions really do count.

Make the Repairs

Your walk through will have highlighted areas that need repairs. Make them now. Don't put it off any longer. Replace broken blinds and furniture. A threadbare carpet is unacceptable.

Buy Whatever You Need

Chapter 5 indicates what each guest room will need. Your walk through will have told you what each guest room already has so now is the time to acquire anything that is missing. Pretty bedding and fresh towels will help make your guest feel comfortable. You will need three sets for each bed, one on the bed, one in the linen cupboard and one in the wash. You may also need to buy new duvets and pillows.

Take a look at your crockery, glasses and cutlery. Are they past their sell by date, chipped, mismatched or inadequate? Get some more. Guests are paying for a stay in a home but they do expect to be warm and comfortable.

Spend A Night

When your room is set up and you feel ready, spend a night in the room. It is amazing what you will learn. Sockets too far from the mirror, street light shines through the window, the mattress is uncomfortable and so on. If you can, ask a friend to stay the night as a Secret Shopper guest. Ask them to give you an honest opinion and then act on it.

If you are not comfortable in the room then your guest won't be either.

Take Photos

Last but not least, take new photos that you can use in your advertising material. At least one per guest room, one of the outside front and back, one of the kitchen, one of the dining room and one of the lounge. These will form your shop window and will either entice a potential guest to contact you or will cause said guest to move on to somewhere else.

To summarise, you will need to be all things to all people. Some of the roles you will be able to give to others, like hiring a cleaner or laundry service. Knowing a local handyman will be useful, but if all else fails, YouTube can instruct you in most repairs. You will need to be a cook, a counsellor, a guide, grammar aide and a nurse. A qualified accountant, however, is a must.

Be proud of yourself and your home.

Call To Action

- Develop an outline business plan

- Begin to plan how much you will charge. You can always change it later

- Estimate what your expenses will be

- Determine whether to expect a security deposit or holding fees

- Identify the purpose of occupancy levels and their use to your business

- Prepare a diary system that is suitable for your business

- Create an information sheet for your guest rooms

- Do the necessary cleaning and maintenance

- Buy any necessary equipment or furniture

- Spend a night in a completed guest room

- Take a final set of photos that you can use to advertise your homestay

CHAPTER 7

LEGAL ISSUES

There are lots of legal issues that you should consider but they are not nearly as complicated as you may think. I am confident that the information in this book is correct at this time. But the legal world is ever evolving so it would be sensible to visit the relevant websites to check for any changes.

Insurance

You will need buildings and contents insurance that will cover any damage caused by a guest or to anything owned by a guest. Check with your current provider. It is likely that you are already covered but if not call them to amend your insurance. Remember to use terms like "lodgers" and "homestay guests". You are not renting out rooms or renting to tenants.

You will also need to check that you have public liability insurance in case one of your guests has an accident in your home and is injured.

Tax

You will need to visit an accountant to get the best possible advice. The information here is a guide only.

Open a separate bank account for your homestay income and out goings. I use my debit card to pay for everything so that there is a record of every item of expenditure, even down to a pint of milk.

Keep all your receipts, sorted into months so that you or your accountant can fill in your tax return more easily.

Use a cash book or spreadsheet to record everything and to summarise your monthly expenses. This will help your accountant but will also show you where you are spending your money. It will also help you to see trends and plan for the future.

The tax rules are complicated and only a qualified accountant can advise you.

Local authority

- **Planning permission**

  If your home is your primary residence while you have guests staying you do not need to have planning permission to let rooms in your home.

- **Housing benefit**

  If you receive housing benefit and are one of the many people who have had their benefits cut by the loss of the spare room subsidy you may be thinking about using your spare room to help make up the difference.

  You are allowed to do this and many councils will actively encourage this. You will lose a proportion of your housing benefit but will still be better off.

- **Council tax**

  Council tax may be affected if you are currently receiving a single person subsidy. If you are paying the full council tax then you will not have to pay anymore.

  If you receive a subsidy and your guests are under eighteen or students in full-time education then you will not lose the subsidy but you must inform the council.

  It is your responsibility to inform the council of any changes.

Guest Rights

- **License to Occupy**

  As a homestay, your guest will have what is called a license to occupy. They will not have a tenancy. You will retain rights to your entire home with unrestricted movement. A tenant would have the right to keep you out of the space that they occupy; they have exclusive use under the law.

  Holding a licence to occupy means that under the law the guest is termed an excluded occupier. This means the guest has only a few limited rights and you will not need to apply to a court for eviction.

  Excluded occupiers share their accommodation with the landlord or host.

- **Rent book**

  No rent book is required for excluded occupiers but you should always provide a receipt when taking money. Keep records for yourself as well.

- **Your access rights**

  You will retain the legal right to enter a guest's room at any time. It is your home after all. Obviously, this should be for a specific purpose such as cleaning, emptying bins, repairs etc. You would need to give twenty-four hours written notice to a tenant but a homestay guest is acting as a member of your household.

  Your guests do not have the right to insist they have a lock on their door. If they insist then homestay is not the correct environment for them.

  I do not have locks on my guest rooms as it is a home, not a business premises and these are guests not tenants. However, if you want to have locks on their doors you have the right to retain a key.

Fire Safety

This is not intended to quote the full extent of the law regarding fire safety. I am giving you a broad outline and information on where to get further help.

For the safety of everyone in your home, you should carry out a fire risk assessment. This is a structured way of looking at the potential risks in your home.

1. Identify the fire hazards

2. Identify the people at risk

3. Evaluate, remove, reduce and protect from risk

4. Record, plan, inform, instruct and train

5. Review the assessment periodically

UK fire safety legislation requires that 'suitable and sufficient' fire risk assessment must be carried out.

You can find a fire risk assessment tool online on the Visit Britain website at https://www.visitbritain.org/pink-book/fire-risk-assessment-tool

There is also help from the government to do a fire risk assessment. There is a template that you can use.

https://www.gov.uk/government/publications/do-you-have-paying-guests

Work out how your guests would escape if a fire started. Draw up an emergency evacuation plan and display a copy in each guest room.

Your kitchen is always a potential fire risk. Have a good look around and identify any hazards.

- Electrical equipment such as tumble dryer, cooker, fridge, kettle, microwave

- Lighting, floor, cabinets, floor level

- Hanging cables are a potential fire risk but also a trip hazard

- Cloths too close to the cooker

- Furnishings

- Flammable liquids such as cleaning products

- Wood panelling

- Curtains

When you have identified any risks you must work out how to remove or reduce them.

For example:

- If you have curtains in the kitchen that could blow near a cooking pot, you could remove them or replace with a bind.

- Frayed electrical cords should be replaced; tumble dryer filters cleaned out and so on.

- Smoking should definitely not be allowed in bedrooms.

Make sure that you have a fire extinguisher and a fire blanket in the kitchen. You will also need a smoke alarm and a CO2 alarm.

It is a good idea to do a fire risk assessment annually as things in your home will change. Your local Fire Safety Officer is a good source of help as well.

Fire Certificate

You do not need to have a fire certificate unless:

- You have more than six people staying in the home

- Some of the accommodation is above the first floor level

- Some of the accommodation is below the ground floor level

Food Hygiene Certificate

If you are going to provide food or drink for your guests you must be aware of the potential threats to your guests from illnesses or allergies.

Fundamentally, the food hygiene legislation states that:

- You should not provide food that is unsafe or unfit for human consumption

- Food must not be stored at unsafe temperatures

- There must be no cross contamination of food

You must comply with the legislation. But please don't panic, it's not complicated.

Your local council has a department with food safety inspectors that regulates and gives advice to help with these issues.

It is worth signing up for a food hygiene course either locally or online. There are three levels of Food Hygiene Certification. Level 2 is for people who work in a kitchen preparing and serving food. These courses will give you lots of information about storing, preparing and cooking food.

You have a duty to your guests to keep them healthy.

Cleaning: You must keep the area where food is stored, prepared and served clean at all times. Anything that comes into contact with food must also be scrupulously clean.

Cooking: You must ensure that food is cooked to the correct temperature and for the correct length of time.

Refrigeration: Freezing or chilling at the correct temperature is imperative to prevent the growth of bacteria.

Contamination: Don't allow fresh and cooked food to come into contact when you store it. This will allow bacteria to spread. You must also be aware of cross contamination concerning allergies for example peanuts or gluten.

TV and Music Licence

If you live in your home and have less than fifteen TVs or other viewing devices then you do not need a special licence. Therefore, a homestay is very unlikely to need anything other than the normal TV licence.

Nevertheless it is advisable to check with the TV licencing authority. Details of their website are in the appendices.

In 2010 a change was made to the legislation for playing copyrighted music. If you live on the premises and have no more than three guest rooms then a Performing Arts licence is not required.

Registration and Data Protection

You must keep records for twelve months of everyone who stays in your home if they are over sixteen years old. This is old legislation (1972) and may be repealed soon. In the meantime, you must record your guest's full name and nationality. You are not legally required to keep information about their address or telephone number. You must record passport details (or Identity Cards) if the guest is not British, Irish or from a Commonwealth country.

The format of your register doesn't matter. You could use a visitor's book from a stationers or a basic exercise book from the supermarket. Police show little or no interest but that could change.

If your guest has come to you through a language school or homestay agent then the information will be recorded on their system for you.

As you are holding information about guests the General Data Protection Regulation (GDPR), which came into force on 25th May 2018, applies.

GDPR applies to everyone holding information about someone else but it is fundamentally very simply with regards to homestay.

You do not need to notify the Information Commission Office (ICO):

- If the information that you hold is for advertising and marketing only

- If you do not disclose the information to a third party without the consent of the guest

- If the information is held for accounting purposes

The Information Commissioner's Office (ICO) has produced several resources to help businesses comply with GDPR. Their website can be found in the appendix.

Call To Action

- Check your insurance cover. Purchase a new policy if necessary

- If you intend to take occasional guests from a language school you will not need an accountant, otherwise hire an accountant and get advise specific to your needs

- Check with your local authority if you are in receipt of benefits

- Undertake a fire risk assessment

- Apply online for a food hygiene course if you have decided to do it

- Identify the GDPR requirements necessary to your business

CHAPTER 8

PUBLIC AREAS

When you decide to allow guests into your home most of it will become a public area. This is a simple fact and you must be happy with that decision. That doesn't mean you can't have your own private areas or that guests can or will start looking through your drawers. To my knowledge, in the seven years I have been doing this, I have never experienced anyone that has over stepped the mark. I have a study, a work room and a bedroom and no one has entered any of them without my express permission and I have occasionally left money lying around and it has never been taken. Not that I am suggesting it won't happen but I firmly believe people are good and I have yet to be proved wrong.

That said, you must be prepared for the occasional lapse and for the idea that if you really want something to be private then it is your responsibility to protect it. I spent years working in an office and left all sorts of personal things in my drawers from chocolate to money to papers. If they "walked" then it really was my own fault but again, it almost never happened.

Except for pens, they have a will of their own and no matter what you do pens run away all by themselves. Presumably, they set up home with the odd socks and happily raise a family of pocks and sens!

I do have a large filing cabinet in my office with a lock. I keep my accounting information in it.

Entrance Hall

Keep your hall well-lit and uncluttered. Guests arrive and leave with suitcases. Obvious I know but it is surprising how much room they take up in a standard British hall.

I used to have a pretty wooded bench in the hall when I lived alone. I placed my shoes underneath when I came home and hung my coat on a hook on the wall.

About a year after I started taking guests, I was frustrated that the hall always seemed messy, particularly with discarded shoes. I went to my favourite store, Ikea and came back with a semi-circular white metal hall shelf and coat rack and a tall white shoe store. The wooden bench found its way to the conservatory and the coat rack and shoe store took its place. I still have them now and they are perfect for my home. Sometimes things are trial and error, what works for me may not work for you.

On arrival, I show the guests the shoe cupboard. I don't tell them "no shoes in my house" but they see me without shoes and know about the rack and hey presto problem avoided.

Bicycle helmets and umbrellas sit neatly on top of the shelf and coats hang contentedly from the hooks. No maintenance required.

The shoe cupboard hides away unsightly and sometimes smelly shoes and the top provides a perfect resting place for any mail that arrives for the guests. If you only have short term guests then the mail is rarely an issue, but university students often get mail.

If you have a porch you could choose to keep shoes and coats out there, but again, I would urge you to keep the porch clean and tidy as it is the guest's entrance to your domain and will set the precedent for how they view your home and also how they treat it. If your home is untidy, guests will take that as a cue that they don't need to be tidy.

Lounge

I have a decent sized lounge and a couple of years ago I bought a six seater corner sofa. This allows everyone to sit on it when necessary but also makes the room look less cluttered than a traditional three piece suite.

Actually I find that my guests only use my lounge occasionally. Sometimes I suggest a film night and we watch a Sky Cinema movie and eat popcorn or I splash out on a takeaway. Guests these days very rarely travel without a laptop or smart device and tend to watch movies in their rooms.

I also have a great deal of books. Last time I moved house my family said it was the last time they would help me move if I didn't shed some books. I did. It broke my heart about four years ago as I got rid of over 300 and left myself with only a little over 200. I counted them again about a month ago and somehow, the book fairies are to blame, I am back up to 482. About 20% are fiction and the rest are crafts, esoteric, history, travel, language, conspiracy theory, business and so on and so on. My guests often browse and usually find something interesting to read. They also sometimes leave their own books behind when they are too heavy for the plane.

Set your rules. If you don't want guests in your lounge you don't have to allow it. I would suggest that you put a TV in their bedroom if that is the case.

I had an elderly couple from Australia who stayed for four nights a couple of years ago and they very much made themselves at home with their feet up on my sofa. I actually liked the fact that they felt so comfortable in my home that they were able to act accordingly. You may not, however. Your house, your rules!

Dining room

What you do here will probably depend on the style of your home:

- Separate lounge, dining room and kitchen

- Lounge/diner and kitchen

- Lounge and kitchen/diner

Mine is open plan with lounge, dining room and kitchen all open to each other. It is a great layout for conversation but not so good for shutting yourself away. You simply have to work with what you have.

Every evening before I go to bed I lay the table for breakfast. I tell the students when they arrive where they can make toast and tea or coffee but put everything else on the table. Milk stays in the fridge obviously.

Place the toaster and kettle in an easily visible and accessible place. I tell the guests that they can help themselves to breakfast whenever they like. This makes them feel at ease with when they want to get up. Be it 3am or 10am. I suggest that you do clear breakfast away at some point as it looks messy if you don't. On their first morning, I try to be up before them so I can remind them of where things are and I usually say that I clear away about 11am. However, I tell them where everything is so if they want breakfast after I have cleared away they can still get it. Your house, your rules!

I lay up for dinner usually around 6pm and we eat at 7pm. But you must decide what works best for you. For a couple of years, I worked in an office whilst running the homestay and finished work at 5pm. On the thirty minute drive home I was planning what to have for dinner so when I got in I hit the ground running.

Always eat at the table with your guests and do your best to make it the centre of their homestay experience. In my home, we eat and talk and generally set the world to rights. It makes everyone feel cared for and their opinion valued and gives lots of practice at speaking and expressing themselves in English.

It can be challenging and tiring, keeping the conversation flowing, making everyone feel included and translating between two guests of different cultures whose accents are proving problematic. I love it.

Kitchen

My kitchen is the only area that I am a bit OCD about. I don't like people using my cooker or my cooking utensils. I am not a brilliant cook and I don't have world class equipment but they are mine and I don't like others using them. I also don't like people under my feet when I am cooking, I get stressed. I don't know why, that's just the way it is. My house, my rules!

VAT

When you are planning your homestay business think about how you feel about things. Stand quietly in your kitchen for a few minutes and really look and imagine how you will feel and how you can make it work for you. Head off the problem before it happens.

If you have a separate kitchen you can ban guests from it completely if you prefer. Stick a sign on the door that says Private. It would not be my choice as, for me, guests are just that, guests. The fact that they are paying makes no difference. They are paying for a homely experience and signs saying keep out are not very homely. Again the simplest way is to head off the problem by keeping the door shut. It is very unlikely they will walk in without knocking first so you could go to the door and stay in the door way to discuss the issue and shut it again.

As I said, my ground floor is pretty much all open plan but there is a clearly defined kitchen area and, on reflection, the area around the cooker is my no-go area. Guests often sit at the breakfast bar to chat while I am cooking but if they come into MY area, I simply suggest that they might like to take a seat at the breakfast bar. This faces into the cooking area but has the advantage of a wide worktop breakfast bar in between so my personal space is not impinged upon.

Other areas of the kitchen I have no problem with. I show guests where plates, cutlery and mugs are kept. I show them how to make tea and get milk from the fridge.

If you want to keep guests out of the kitchen you could get a small desktop fridge for the dining room. Keep crockery and cutlery in there along with a toaster and a kettle. If I had a separate kitchen I think this would be my choice but it could take on a guest house feel rather than a homestay. You must ask yourself if that matters to you.

Bathroom

Sharing a bathroom with strangers can be problematic. It really must be clean at all times. Bed and breakfasts these days simply have to have en-suite rooms but then have to charge accordingly. But your home is not a bed and breakfast, it's your home. You can certainly charge more for an en-suite room but it is very unlikely that your home has many of these going spare. There is probably only one, so don't feel bad about keeping it for you.

So how can you make it work?

- All bathrooms and cloakrooms MUST have a locking door. If you don't have a lock then fit a bolt before a guest arrives

- I have learnt over the years that the bathroom needs to be depersonalised if you are going to have multiple guests using it. That doesn't mean it can't be pretty, just that it shouldn't have personal items like a tooth brush, towels, dressing gown, hair brush etc.

- If guests leave things in the bathroom, simply remove them and place then outside the guest's room

- You will need to have a bath mat and hand towel available for general use and these should be changed every day

- Keep the bathroom spotless

- Use pump action hand soap rather than cakes of soap which harbour a multitude of germs

Garden

If you don't have a garden then the guests can't share it, but you may have outside areas such as a back yard or a balcony. Same rules apply as everywhere else, clean and depersonalised.

I don't allow smoking in my home but I allow it outside. If you choose to do this you must make sure ashtrays are available and are emptied every day.

Call To Action

- Declutter

- Decide how you want to deal with the dining room and kitchen

- Determine how you want your shared bathroom to work. Put up signs if you wish too

- Examine your garden

CHAPTER 9

FOOD

Food is always something that I am asked about. Most commonly "how do you cope with all those different types of food?" The answer, of course, is "I don't".

There are two types of guests. Firstly, British people looking for something cheap and so a good, home cooked British meal is always welcome. Secondly, foreigners looking to experience British food and culture. So why on earth would I try to cook authentic Korean food for someone from Korea?

No, the answer is always normal, everyday British food. Shepherd's pie, bangers and mash, fish and chips, beef casserole, roast. The British also regularly eat spaghetti, curries, pizza and lasagne, so serve this as well. Don't try to cook authentic foreign food just because you have someone from that country. In the appendices you will find a four week menu which I follow carefully when I am a bit short of money or imagination and have to plan ahead carefully.

I give a free evening meal for my guests. I don't charge extra for it, but obviously, the price is built in.

> VAT
>
> By advertising dinner as free, the guest feels they are getting a good deal

I am a bit of a control freak which is why I run the business this way and don't simply let out a room.

When I started out, I stated in my advertisements that dinner was included. I then had a series of difficult conversations when guests wanted a discount because they didn't want to eat my food and I didn't want to allow them the use of my kitchen to cook for themselves. I changed my advert to say free dinner. You can't discount something that is free in the first place. It's a bit like the all-inclusive holidays that are destroying the local economies in seaside resorts.

For me, this is a better option though it does tie me down a bit. So think it through before you make a decision.

There are times due to family commitments that I am not available to sit down and eat dinner with my guests. I try not to do this often but my family comes first so I have to deal with it. I still cook, lay the table etc. I plate the food with a cover and put it on the table. I warn the group the night before that I will not be with them and that they should warm their dinner in the microwave. My home is not a restaurant with waitress service and the meal is free. No-one has ever complained.

To Cook Or Not To Cook

Most colleges, language schools and any other groups that have a homestay programme will almost certainly expect you to provide a hot meal every day and many will expect a packed lunch too. When you make contact, be sure to establish exactly what their requirements are. The following advice is based upon your guests booking privately rather than through an organisation.

- **Catering**

    Whether you cook for your guests is your choice. I do it because for long term guests the alternative is self-catering.

    I do allow guests to reheat food in the microwave. If they are going to come home late or I am out, their dinner is on a plate and they are free to reheat. I also supply "oats so simple" for breakfast so they heat it themselves in the microwave.

    I don't provide lunch for anyone unless it is a pre-booked and paid for packed lunch. Lunch is a commitment too far for me I am afraid. Occasionally guests do heat something in the microwave but I don't find it particularly intrusive so I don't object. Your house, your rules!

    I do keep the bottom shelf of my fridge available for guests to leave their own things. There is never very much but sometimes individuals bring items home to take the next day for lunch. There are also occasions when guests want something specific like soy based snacks or pickled cucumber. One of my guests wanted to make her own sandwiches for lunch so she bought the ingredients on a Sunday and made a weeks' worth of sandwiches that I allowed her to store in my freezer. I wasn't actually very happy with this as it took up quite a lot of space and didn't seem very cost or time effective for her, but still, service is so service so I acquiesced.

- **Self-catering**

    As a host I simply don't want other people cooking in my kitchen, making a mess and not cleaning up. I am very capable of making my own mess thank you!

I find others cooking around me very stressful and I quickly get irritated. I am not being fair I know.

So if you don't want to cook for your guests the alternative is to allow them to forage for their own sustenance. Some will get out pots and pans, some will go to a café/restaurant and others will get takeaways.

Decide which is the lesser of the evils. Then make it clear what you expect of them.

Remember to consider clear up, food storage, equipment usage and cooking smells.

Types of Diets

For the next few pages, I am assuming you have decided to take the nurturing role of a mother hen and cook. I do enjoy cooking and the empty nest syndrome meant no-one wanted my food. Say ahhh.

Quickly I learned that people want their dietary needs catered for. I didn't initially advertise that I could or would cook different types of food. Then I realised that I really should. If you are willing to provide this service it will attract more guests to your homestay.

VAT

If you have a strong view on something state it clearly in your advertisement; what you will and will not do and what you will and will not allow.

It is, however, illegal to be discriminatory of race, sexual orientation, religion or disability.

- ## Vegan

One of my first guests, Vittoria from Italy, emailed me on the day before her arrival, giving me flight details and arrival times. At the end, she added a PS. "I am Vegan". She was coming for a year and I had a full meltdown when I read the email. I have never cooked for a vegan; vegetarians are not a problem, but vegan......really. I raced into town the next morning and found several vegan recipe books.

After a few days I settled in and the fear dropped away. The supermarkets now are much more helpful and Quorn have recently started a vegan range, but then it was much more difficult. Holland and Barret are a good source of special foods but also for help and advice.

I learnt a lot and even discovered in an episode of "Walking Dead" that you can replace eggs in a cake with apple sauce. Yes, it is a good question, why were they making cakes in the middle of a zombie apocalypse. But they really did, Carol arrived in Alexandria and wanted to make a cake but they didn't have any eggs. I checked it out and it's true. Replace each egg for the 60g of the cheapest possible apple sauce. Cheap is not because I am mean, it means there are fewer lumps of solid apple. The cakes rise perfectly and do not taste of apple. I don't know the chemistry behind it but it works.

Other things that caught me out were honey, gelatine and some pasta. Vegans don't eat anything that emanates from an animal.

I must have done something right as Vittoria stayed for five years and has grown into a beautiful and talented woman who I am proud to claim as my friend.

- ## Vegetarian

The popularity of vegetarianism has risen so much that I can confidently say sooner rather than later you will need to cater for a vegetarian. It really isn't difficult or expensive these days. Quorn is an excellent product and I usually simply replace the meat with the Quorn equivalent. Peppers, aubergines or squash stuffed with rice, mushroom risotto, omelettes and frittatas are all excellent standbys. Vegetable curry or nut roast is also great.

- **Gluten free**

Gluten free cooking needs more care. Gluten intolerance is a problem for your guest but an allergy could be very serious. The supermarkets all sell gluten free products now but they are certainly more expensive. Get yourself a good book and read up on it.

For example, I keep a separate toaster in a box and bring it out when necessary. Using normal bread creates breadcrumbs and putting a slice of gluten free bread in the toaster after will contaminate the bread and could make your guest ill.

Breadcrumbs on commercial chicken or fish will contain gluten so you can't use them either.

- **Pork free**

Various religions object to eating pork as it is considered an unclean meat. In the Britain of the 21st century pork is raised disease and parasite free and is no longer the health risk it was in the past. However, you may have guests that will not eat pork despite modern farming methods.

Initially, this doesn't sound too bad, but when you consider how many things contain pork it is not so simple. Roast pork, gammon, bacon, sausages, scotch eggs, ham and pork pies for example. I don't generally cook a separate meal for a guest with a pork free diet; I simply give everyone no pork that day. This strategy is fine for a week or two but then I have to do a different meal for that guest so that the rest of us can have our pork fix.

- **Halal**

Halal is Arabic for permissible. Halal food adheres to Islamic law, as defined in the Qur'an.

The Islamic form of slaughtering animals or poultry involves killing through a cut to the jugular vein, carotid artery and windpipe. Animals must be alive and healthy at the time of slaughter and all the blood is drained from the carcass. During the process, a Muslim will recite a prayer.

You can buy halal meat from the major supermarkets these days.

- **Soya milk**

I started buying soya milk when Vittoria (my Vegan guest) moved in. Personally, I don't like it but many do. I have been told by various Chinese guests that there is something in many Chinese constitutions that makes them intolerant to cow's milk. Therefore I usually have soya milk available. You can easily get the long life variety to hold in store.

Meals

- **Breakfast**

It is a common misconception amongst foreigners that we eat a full, cooked English breakfast every day. Some are horrified at the thought whilst others are excited at the idea.

I don't offer a cooked breakfast. I don't charge enough for the night rate and as most of my guests are long term they would die of heart failure after a few weeks. Cooked breakfast should be a treat for high days and holidays.

> VAT
>
> You can legitimately offer the real British breakfast that real British people eat every day. Cereal and toast.

A cooked breakfast would mean I have to get up and cook it to suit my guest's timetable. A light normal breakfast allows me to lay the table the night before and the guests can help themselves whenever they are ready.

The table contains

o   A tray with jams, marmalade, chocolate spread, marmite and lemon curd

o   Butter or spread

o   Orange juice and cranberry juice

o   A box with instants oats in various flavours

o   Three or four boxes of assorted cereals and muesli

I set each place with a cereal bowl, spoon, side plate, knife and a juice glass. When the guest arrives I show them where the tea/coffee making things are and also the toaster which is located on the work top next to the microwave. I should point out that I have an open plan kitchen diner so kettle, microwave and toaster, whilst technically in the kitchen, are easily accessible.

If you have a separate kitchen you may want to consider putting the toaster in the dining room for ease of use.

- **Lunch**

  I don't serve lunch. The day time is mine and preparing lunch would tie me down too much. Most guests are out all day or busy studying in their rooms. However, I did hit on another small income stream by preparing a packed lunch for a price. The local shops do a three item meal deal for between £3 and £3.50. So I decided to do something similar. I have the lunch offer printed in each room. I charge £3.00 for five items. See the appendix for a copy.

  o   Sandwich or baguette

  o   Packet of crisps

  o   Bottle of water

  o   Piece of fruit

  o   Chocolate biscuit

- **Dinner**

  For me, dinner is the main event of the day. Guests come in from work, study, training, sightseeing etc. And want to share their day's experiences. Someone to say "well done" or "poor you" goes a very long way. Through trial and error, I found that having dinner at 7pm every night suits most people and situations. It is late enough to get through their day and travel but early enough to allow them to go out for the evening after. Consistency is important as it allows everyone to plan around it.

  Let me say something about my family at this point. I live alone but two of my three children live close by. I have trained them to know that I am 'working' between 6pm and 8pm. This limits the phone calls and pop-ins to times when I can comfortably be with them without detracting from my guests.

It is important that your family understand that you are taking this seriously and that you are at work. They wouldn't pop into your office or shop and expect you to stop work so they must be helped to understand that your time with your guests is part of your job.

Don't provide a menu that guests can choose from. This is your home not a hotel. Think of it as an old fashioned traditional home. Mum chooses what to eat, shops for it and cooks it. The family eats, smiles and says thank you.

Do ask guests if there is anything they don't like and try to accommodate their need.

I find it best to place food in dishes in the centre of the table and the guests can help themselves. In your own family, you know who will eat what and how much but with guests you rarely know.

I give my guests a two course meal every night. Either soup and bread followed by a main course, or a main course followed by a dessert. I always lay the table in a semi-formal way. I do, however, use paper napkins from Asda or Ikea. Fabric napkins generate too much laundry.

When I serve soup I use the part cooked baguettes which create a nice smell and the guests get nice warm fresh baked bread. They keep in the cupboard if unopened for ages and are really good value.

Sometimes a guest will be late for dinner but would still like to eat. I plate the meal for them to reheat when they arrive. I leave their place set at the table until they have eaten.

I do try to work out a varied menu so that long term guests aren't always eating the same food. It's up to you of course. If you make a menu it does help with shopping and budgeting but it isn't necessary and even though I have one I frequently ignore it and cook what I feel like today. Remember it's your home, your rules!

Food Hygiene

Most people keep a clean house and a clean kitchen and in this section I am not implying otherwise. However, there are a few things that you need to consider.

As you will be supplying food, even if it is only breakfast, you will need to make sure that food storage, preparation and serving is scrupulously clean.

If you can, I suggest that you do an online food certificate. It takes a couple of hours and costs very little. Search for one that suits you and gives an immediate downloadable certificate that you can display on your kitchen wall. There are also many colleges and private companies all over the country that offer lessons if you are feeling less confident.

Remember that you are cooking for others and imagine how you would feel if someone got food poisoning. The following is just a way to focus your attention.

Fridge

- Always keep it wiped clean and throw away food that is open or out of date

- Keep cooked food covered

- Keep uncooked meat covered and on a shelf underneath any cooked or fresh food. You don't want any fresh meat juices dripping onto food that will be served without cooking first. It could be a real germ fest

- Your fridge should be at or below 4°C. If you leave the door open for too long the temperature will rise and may affect the food

- Your freezer should be at or below -18°C. Again leaving the door open or allowing it to freeze up could affect the food

- Fridge and freezer thermometers are quite cheap and you may be surprised at how leaving a door open for a short time raises the temperature

Work tops

- Always wipe up spills as soon as they happen. Wipe the surface with a clean cloth or impregnated wipe

- If the mess was made by raw meat make sure you use a disinfectant spray

- Obviously the same applies to floor spills

- When you have finished cooking, make sure that you wash every surface thoroughly

Microwave

- The microwave is a place that often gets overlooked. It is a great place for germs to congregate. One of the common places to miss is the inside roof. How it all gets up there is anyone's guess but it can get pretty bad.

- Using white vinegar is a cheap and easy way to clean the microwave.

   1. Half fill a bowl with water and add a tablespoon of white vinegar

   2. Put the bowl on the glass plate in the microwave

   3. Turn it on for around five minutes. This will create steam that will loosen the stuck on mess

   4. Take the bowl out and use a dry cloth or kitchen paper to wipe around the sides, top and bottom

    5.   Wash the glass plate in the sink or dishwasher

o   If you don't have white wine vinegar you can use a lemon cut in half and placed in a bowl with a small amount of water.

o   Don't use abrasive cleaners on the inside of the microwave and do not under any circumstances, ever use a metal based scrubber. If there is residue left behind after the clean up the microwave will spark and may catch fire.

Floors

- Sweep and wash your kitchen floor every day. It will look better and guests will be quick to notice messy floors and may not feel comfortable

- Always wipe up spills as soon as they happen

- If the mess was made by raw meat make sure you use a disinfectant spray

- If you have animals make sure they are kept away from the food preparation area

Wash your hands

- Always wash your hands before you start preparing food as it will help to stop germs getting into the food

- Always wash your hands when you finish preparing food to stop germs from the food spreading to other areas of your home

- To prevent germs being transferred from uncooked meat onto fresh food or utensils, wash your hands frequently during the food preparation process if you have handled meat or poultry

- Dry your hands on a towel, not on the cloth that you use to dry the dishes

Tea cloths and dish clothes

- Use a clean cloth at the beginning of every day. Bacteria grow very quickly

- You will need to have plenty of cloths available

- Wash the cloths on a hot wash

- Dish cloths even though thoroughly washed can still look grubby. I leave mine to soak in half water half bleach for an hour or so in the kitchen sink. This has the added advantage of bleaching the sink and later the drain when you have finished

Dishwasher

- Use a dishwasher cleaner at least once a month

- Wipe around the seals after every use

- Clean out the filter after every use

Kitchen bins

- Empty every day. I do mine last thing before I go to bed so that things don't fester overnight

- Wipe out the bin before you put in a new bin liner. It's amazing how dirty they can get even with a liner

Food preparation

- Wash your hands regularly

- Defrosting meat. You must take care when you defrost frozen meat. I always used to take food out of the freezer and put it on a plate in the kitchen, cover it and walk away. However, germs will quickly multiply at room temperature. The better way is either in the fridge or on the defrost setting of the microwave followed by immediate use

- Never defrost meat in a bowl of water. The result will be highly potent bacteria based soup!

Chopping boards

- Keep separate boards for meat, fish and fresh food to prevent cross contamination

- There are many companies that sell sets of different coloured chopping boards so that you can assign a different colour to each food type

- I know many people use wooden boards but they really are a breeding ground for germs. Personally, I prefer glass boards which can be easily washed in the dish washer. They do have the disadvantage of blunting knives however

Freezing food

Never put hot food directly into the freezer, cool it down first. Hot food will raise the temperature of the freezer and allow bacteria to grow.

Cooking

The main thing to think about when cooking is that all food is cooked to the correct temperature and for the correct length of time.

Storing

- After food has been cooked, any leftovers must be cooled and stored in the fridge to stop or slow down the growth of bacteria

- Do not leave food out on the worktops at room temperature

- Cross contamination is a serious problem. Allowing uncooked meat to come into contact with fresh food is a recipe for disaster

- Beware of peanuts. Some people have severe allergies. I heard of a gentleman who had to be taken to hospital after eating a ham sandwich. The work surface had previously been used to make a peanut butter sandwich

- If you have a guest who is a Coeliac, you will need wheat free bread and a toaster dedicated to this bread type only

Call To Action

- Understand the value of ordinary, everyday British cooking to a homestay guest

- Differentiate between different dietary types

- Read up on what is required and unacceptable for each of the different diet types

- Understand the importance of allergies and intolerances and how this may impact on your cooking

- Demonstrate an understanding of food hygiene principles

CHAPTER 10

ADVERTISING

So now you are thoroughly familiar with your home and location. You know how you want to run your business, what services you are going to provide and what you are going to charge.

All you are missing is guests.

You need to reach as many people as possible and with the digital environment in which we now live you can reach out right across the world. Gone are the days of putting a postcard in the local shop saying "room available". Of course, you can still do that if you want to. A stray Japanese tourist may be walking down the street and just happen to need a bed for the night but I wouldn't count on it if I were you.

So you will need to let the world know that you are available to meet their every need. You need to advertise.

Consider where you are going to advertise and what you are going to say in the adverts.

Where To Advertise

The internet can be a great source of information.

Language schools

Search for language schools in your area and then call them. Ask if they have a homestay programme.

Colleges

Search for colleges in your area that have an international programme. Call them and ask if they provide homestay for their students.

University

Most universities provide lists of accommodation to their students. Apply to the local university to be included on the list.

Social media

Set up a social media page advertising your business. Ask your friends to like and share the page.

Word of mouth

Contact other hosts in your area. Often hosts pass guests on to other hosts if they are unable to take a guest for a specific time.

Web sites

You can set up your own website or advertise on existing third party sites. Or, of course, do both.

Your own site can be quite easy to set up and relatively inexpensive to run. However, getting it seen by the right people is more problematic. High placement on Google or other search engines can be extremely expensive.

A third party site such as Homestay.com, Airbnb.co.uk or SpareRoom.co.uk is already set up for advertising and will help to create your pages for you. They take bookings for you and notify you of the details. Generally, they charge a fee of around 15%. SpareRoom works in a slightly different way as it expects single rather than multiple ongoing bookings.

Advert Contents

Even if you are not going to use a third party site it is still worth looking at how other people advertise. You will learn a lot from this exercise.

Thinking about your own business, consider what will make you stand out to a potential guest. What makes you different or better than your competitors? This will be your Unique Selling Point (USP).

You will need a description of your homestay, what you offer, where you are located and how much you charge. Make it as warm and friendly as possible. You can see mine in the appendix.

Include at least one photograph for each of your guest rooms and one of the front of your home. You can display more of course.

If you have your own website or social media page, adding and managing an availability calendar is complicated. You can simply say that guests should call or message you for availability.

If you advertise on Homestay.com or Airbnb.co.uk, they will manage your bookings diary for you. You can still blank out dates that you don't want to take guests or times when you have bookings from another source.

Business Cards

Business cards are a cheap investment and you can make them yourself if you have a computer and business card stock. If not, a small local printing business will create them for you or use an online supplier such as Vistaprint.

Business cards can be useful on a number of occasions:

- Give them to potential guests so that they can call you when they are ready

- Give them to current guests so that they have your address and number in case of an emergency

- Give them to departing guests so that they can give them out to friends who may want to visit

- Give them to other homestay hosts. Networking is a very useful way of getting business, making friends and getting tips

- Give them to your family and friends so that they can pass them on

- Hand out some to your local language schools and colleges

Call To Action

- Recognise the need for advertising

- Identify the best areas to advertise in to attract guests that fit your preferred guest type

- Contact local language schools and colleges

- Create an attractive website and social media page

- Describe your homestay, what you offer, where you are located and why a prospective guest would want to stay with you

- Purchase some well-designed business cards

- Examine other host's advertisements

CHAPTER 11

TAKING BOOKINGS

After you have pressed the final button and launched your homestay you will be ready to accept bookings.

Mine was a bumbling start with almost no planning. I learnt on the job but really wish I had had someone to tell me what to do. That, of course, was the motivation for this book.

I found a homestay website almost by accident at around 11 o'clock one Sunday night and started filling in the questionnaire that they presented me with. Then I went to sleep. At 9am the following morning I had my first request. It really was the deep end. But I survived, modified and learned.

My diary system has evolved over the years and I am now quite comfortable with it. You can see a sample in the appendix. However, it has to be something that works for you. Many people prefer a paper diary. If you use a paper one then I would suggest a version with a page per day.

I am a visual person so I colour code everything and like to see the big picture so I use a spread sheet.

The coloured columns show who is sleeping in which room and when the room is empty. So if someone asks to stay for two nights arriving on May 3rd I can instantly see that I only have the London room available for one night on May 4th.

I can offer one night or apologise and decline the booking. For me, it is quick and simple. As most of my guests are long term, on a computer I can quickly fill in all the relevant nights. If it was a paper diary I would have to write the same name in the diary on every page up to 365 times. If you are not expecting long term multiple bookings then a paper diary will be plenty.

Month	Day	Date	Event	Britain	Beach	Butterfly	London
May	Tuesday	1st	**Mum shopping dad to group**	Vittoria	Bernard	Chandler	
May	Wednesday	2nd	Mark arrives	Vittoria	Bernard	Chandler	Mark
May	Thursday	3rd	Dane to work Dad to group	Vittoria	Bernard	Chandler	Mark
May	Friday	4th	Mark leaves	Vittoria	Bernard	Chandler	
May	Saturday	5th	Elodie arrives AF6419 9h40. meal with family	Vittoria	Bernard	Chandler	Elodie
May	Sunday	6th	mum and dad scotts in afternoon	Vittoria	Bernard	Chandler	Elodie
May	Monday	7th		Vittoria	Bernard	Chandler	Elodie

I always highlight the whole row in red if I don't want to have guests for that period. This year I will be closed over Christmas as my guests are all European and will go home. International students from further away often don't go home at all during their stay due to the costs involved so I often have guests over Christmas. Your house, your choice!

Month	Day	Date	Event	Britain	Beach	Butterfly	London
December	Saturday	22nd					
December	Sunday	23rd					
December	Monday	24th					
December	Tuesday	25th					
December	Wednesday	26th					

Using A Third Party Website

If you are using a third party website, all the booking details will be taken care of for you but you will still need your own diary. I often get bookings from alternate sources so I have to regularly synchronise the website diary with my own version. If you don't, you could end up being very embarrassed by double bookings. This has only happened to me once, luckily, and I was able to deal with it by giving up my own room and sleeping in my work room. I sorted it out before either affected guest arrived so they were not aware I had messed it up. I am a great believer in avoiding problems by being proactive but still, we all have to react sometimes.

The booking process begins with an enquiry and you want to do your best to convert the enquiry to a booking. It's all about communication and reassuring your potential guest that you understand their needs and are both willing and able to help them.

Many of the websites take a booking fee from the guests. You don't get this, they keep it. It is usually 15%. If I get the booking from an alternative source I take a non-refundable deposit of 10%

These web sites will send an email and text message direct to your phone when a guest makes an enquiry. This allows you to respond virtually immediately to a request. If you have a face book page for your business, face book will also send you details of an enquiry.

Enquiry Becomes A Booking

Eventually, you will get someone who decides that they do want to stay with you and confirms their booking. This is called a conversion.

Get as much information as you can before they arrive.

- Name

- Contact details

- Date of birth or at least age group

- Email address

- Telephone number

- Room required

- Arrival date

- Departure date

- Dietary requirements

You may decide that you do not want to deal with special diets but if you feel happy too, then try to find out at the time of the booking.

It is unlikely they will know arrival times at the time of booking although I have had a booking where the person arrived a little over an hour later.

Always send a personal confirmation of the booking and include detailed directions and a copy of the invoice so that they clearly know how much they will need to pay on arrival. You can see an example of the invoice that I use in the appendix. It is only a suggestion; use whatever form of invoice will suit you best.

The confirmation should state clearly your terms and conditions. For example cash on arrival, no credit cards, electronic transfer details and your cancellation policy.

> VAT
>
> A week before the guest's arrival send an email asking for their arrival time so that you can be sure to be at home. This also means that you don't have to be at home quietly waiting for the rest of the time.

Make sure you fill in your diary with the booking details. If the booking did not come through your website then make sure you remember to update the website availability so that no-one else can book the room.

Call To Action

- Ensure you have a robust diary even if you are using a third party website to take bookings for you

- Differentiate between an enquiry and a booking. If an enquiry does not convert to a booking then you must try and find out why

- Record details of your guest's booking

- Confirm the booking with the guest using a friendly style

Chapter 12

GUEST ARRIVALS AND DEPARTURES

As a homestay host, you must always be at home when your guest arrives and departs. This is really important. It will set the tone for the whole visit and show your guest that they are a welcome guest in your home.

I offer to pick up or drop off guests from the local airport (it is only a mile away), or from the railway or coach station. It's not mandatory of course but I feel it is a kind thing to do for a foreign visitor. Schools and agencies often do this for you and will drop off at your home.

First Impressions

Before guests can reach your front door though you will have had contact with them via text, email or phone. This will be their real first impression.

If you get an electronic message asking for details and availability respond at the first possible opportunity. Often guests are contacting multiple potential homes and you could easily miss a guest because you don't respond quickly enough.

If they telephone you, it is a bit like a telephone interview and of course, it works both ways.

Always sound cheerful and helpful on the phone. A grumpy host will very rarely translate into a booking. Try and go the extra mile during the conversation and make the potential guest feel that you really care about them and want their visit to be successful.

Always send a confirmation of the booking and include detailed directions.

As your guest walks around the corner, pulls their car onto your drive or gets out of the taxi they will see your home for the first time.

Clean windows, fresh paint, a well-kept front garden and a swept drive all make a great impact.

However, you are not running a five star hotel, it's your home so don't be intimidated into thinking you have to have everything in pristine condition.

VAT

Clean, homely and friendly outweighs everything else.

When you answer the door to your new guest, they get their first impression of you and your home. I love bright colours and butterflies. You can't miss them.

Smile warmly and shake hands, introduce yourself and check their name. You don't want to assume that the man who came to read the electric meter wants a bed for the night!

Some people say that you should have nice smells coming from the kitchen such as fresh coffee or baked bread. As I really detest coffee, if I smelt it on arrival I would definitely be put off and might even turn tail and leave. Fresh bread would attract me but my preference would simply be a fresh clean smell. Your house, your choice!

Welcome

You will probably be feeling a little nervous immediately before a new guest arrives. Someone unknown in your home, will you like them, what if they don't like you, what if their English is very limited? So imagine how stressed your guest will be feeling. A warm and welcoming smile will go a long way to relieving the tension.

Having strangers in your home is uncomfortable so the quicker you turn them into friends the better you will feel. Helping your guests to understand how your household works and the house rules will help this process. It is a two way process however, your guest will have expectations and will have things that they need from you. Communication and mutual respect are key.

Booking In

After a friendly welcome ask for identification. This is a safety measure as you are allowing a stranger full run of your home. Check the ID against the booking form. You could photocopy it or if you have a phone, take a photograph. Assure your guest that it will be deleted after they leave. Also, confirm their leaving date.

Keys

Give your guest their front door key and explain any of the vagaries of your front door. For example, mine is a UPVC double glazed door and you must lift the handle to engage the extra locking mechanisms in the frame before it can be locked. Most British guests have experienced this before so it is not a surprise but many foreigners are bewildered. I had an issue with a couple of students who became very distressed because they couldn't lock my front door when they went out.

It may be that you keep your door locked at all times or just at night or when you go out. When you hand your guest the key, tell them your expectations. It doesn't need to be a big issue, just a simple statement.

Information Sheet

As part of your business planning, you will have created an information sheet. When you prepare the guest's room the information sheet should be in a prominent place. On arrival, go through the information sheet briefly. They will almost certainly want the Wi-Fi information within moments of arrival.

It is also important to point out the emergency card and suggest that they keep it with them at all times. You can see an example of an emergency card in the appendix.

Taking Payment

You will have decided your payment policy when you were planning your business and notified your guest in your confirmation. When they arrive they will be prepared to pay. Sometimes they will need to go to a cash point first; others will already have paid by bank transfer. Don't be shy about asking for payment, have their invoice ready and sign it as paid when you have the money. You must provide a signed receipt.

If you have agreed with your guest to take monthly payments simply confirm this with them on arrival.

If your guest has come from a language school or other agency then they will probably not be making the payment directly to you. The school or agency will have a system which you will be informed of.

Run Through the House Rules

If you have printed your house rules and displayed them, do a quick run through with your guest. Make this as light hearted as possible. The guest should not feel weighed down with rules and regulations.

Take Details

Make sure that you have any relevant information about your guest concerning any medical conditions. You must know what to do and who to call in case of an emergency.

You may need to administer medication in some emergency situations. Asthma and diabetes are just two examples.

Your Home

Guests will need to be able to find their way around your home and also the local area.

- Show the guest to their room and point out anything that you want them to be aware of. I had a broken double glazing window latch once because I didn't realise that the young man would not understand to press the button in before lifting the latch. He forced it and broke something inside the frame. It cost me £65 to get it repaired.

- Mention to them how and when their room will be cleaned and the bedding changed. Let them know what to do about their rubbish. Should they take it to the main bin themselves or will you? I always ask guests to keep their toiletries in their rooms rather than the bathroom. It is tidier but also means that their items won't be inadvertently used by others. Show the information sheet as they will very quickly want the Wi-Fi password.

- Next show them the bathroom. Take the opportunity to discuss any rules or advice. For example, in my home, I always ask guests to leave the bathroom door open when it is not in use. This allows everyone to know instantly when the bathroom is free. It doesn't have to be a rule that is posted on the wall just a comment in passing. But in my home, everyone sticks to it.

- Explain the lack of a waste basket if you decide on this option. You could also mention the disposal of sanitary items if it is appropriate.

- If your taps or plugs are in any way unusual, explain how to use them. Show them where the spare toilet paper is stored; this will avoid embarrassment at a later time.

- I do suggest having a small but friendly sign asking guests to leave the bathroom clean and tidy after use. An unflushed toilet is unpleasant for everyone.

- Suggest that they come down stairs when they have finished unpacking and are ready. I usually offer a cup of tea at this point.

- Show the guest around your kitchen and dining room. Tell them how breakfast works. Don't assume everyone knows how to use a toaster or microwave. Let them know where to find milk and tea making essentials. If you have fruit or cake readily available show them where to get it.

- I usually tell guests that I will explain how to use the washing machine at a later time. Too much information is overwhelming.

- Above all, be patient and show them what to do.

Further Introductions

Before your guest arrives, make sure that you have printed off their bill. It is perfectly normal to expect the guest to pay in full on arrival. However, I do offer options for long term guests.

When they are ready they will come down stairs and you can give them their bill and take the payment. I don't take cards and my adverts make this clear. I do supply details for electronic transfers and often young foreign students are being paid for by their parent from another country. You will need to know your Bank's IBAN and BIC/SWIFT numbers to accept international payments. A quick visit to your bank will provide you with this information.

VAT

If the guest is not British or Northern European always tell them that the water from our taps is good drinking water. We often forget how privileged we are to have this basic amenity. There are a great many countries that have to buy bottled water to drink or use filter jugs. Don't under estimate this

Show your guest around the rest of your home and tell them about the day to day running. Explain about breakfast and dinner. Ask if they have any food preferences.

Ask if they smoke and tell them where they can go if necessary.

I usually tell guests where the nearest shop is for snacks, where they can find a cash point and where the nearest bus stop is.

Area Orientation

For long term guests, I often do a forty-five minute orientation trip in my car. I show them where the bus stop is and how to walk to the university. I often follow the route of the bus into the city and show them where to get on and off the buses. This is very much dependent on the needs of the guest and is aimed at making them independent in the shortest time possible.

On my trip to Mongolia, I was expected to catch a bus every day to the school and the orphanage. It proved to be very simple but initially, no one showed me as they expected me to do it for myself. The buses were clearly numbered and the tickets were all the same price. Simple! No-one spoke English but hey, I am a capable, confident, educated woman. So everything was fine.

I was scared out of my wits.

I experienced so much on that trip and I have learned to empathise with foreigners coming here. We take things for granted and then expect foreigners to know what to do and how to behave. Then say "do you understand?" Is any question more useless?

VAT

Be patient and understanding. With the a few exceptions guests are here to learn and to enjoy their stay. They want to learn about our country and culture. They are not wilfully misunderstanding or being difficult.

You must decide how much of this hands-on nurturing that you want to do. I am naturally a mother hen, but you really don't need to be in order to run a successful homestay. I tend to be proactive but you can equally be reactive, responding to requests rather than anticipating them.

- Some will want to know the location of a church or a mosque; others will want the nearest shopping mall

- You may have a student who will need to register with a doctor or a dentist

- Business persons may need to know how far away a specific site is. They will often have google maps but if not then they may need your help. Be prepared.

- Provide local maps, tourist information and bus schedules

- If your town has a website, list it on your information sheet

Departure

When your guest is ready to leave make sure they have everything with them and that they leave with a smile on their face. You are a successful host if your guest is sad to leave but has enjoyed their stay and will return to their own country with good memories.

Occasionally mail will arrive for a guest that has already left. It is illegal to destroy this. If you know where the guest has gone, or have a mobile number for them then contact them and ask what they want you to do. If you have no idea how to contact the guest then write on the envelope RTS or Return to Sender and put it back in a post box.

A young man had just returned to Japan having stayed with me for a year. He was always short of money and walked everywhere.

He had an Amazon account which I believe his parents paid so there were frequent deliveries of some quite bizarre items like bottled water (I have no idea why). When he left, under his bed we found an opened pack of thirty-two light bulbs, again, I have no idea why. Sadly, we also found an eleven month old cheque for £142. The university had given him a refund on part of his fees. Not having a bank account in the UK he hadn't known what to do with it so had ignored it. It was particularly sad as he had spent a whole year with virtually no money.

> **VAT**
>
> Build up a communication with your guest so that they can ask if they don't understand how to deal with a situation.

Guest Reviews

If your guest has come from a third party web site they will automatically be approached to leave a guest review a few days after the end of their stay. Before they leave your home, it is worth reminding them that this will happen and ask them to please leave a review if they have enjoyed their stay. Every review on the web site is worth its weight in gold. When new guests are looking to book a homestay one of the first things they do is read the reviews.

If the guest has come from a social media site a review request will need to come from you.

Most language schools also ask guests to review their homestay but it is for their own internal use and is not publicised.

Call To Action

- Consider the importance of first impressions

- Recognise the nervousness of guests during the booking in process

- Supply a front door key to every guest

- Assist your guest to navigate your home

- Be clear on any important house rules

- Supply the guest with their information sheet

- Assist your guest with local orientation

- Rehearse your guest departure routine

CHAPTER 13

HOUSE RULES

When I started out I really hated the idea of house rules. It seemed so like the old idea of a seaside landlady. I naively believed that as family homes don't have lists of rules then neither should I. Of course, all families actually do have rules, it's just that we grow up with them and take them for granted.

There are also cultural differences to be taken into account.

Sit for a few moments and consider what things you want people to do or not do when they are in your home.

I don't mean that you should put signs up everywhere. Communication is the easiest and best way to problem solve. Most issues can be dealt with tactfully or by example. I am always fascinated by how I have never asked anyone to help lay the table or to clear it during or after a meal, yet it happens every time. One person did it one day so the others at the table joined in. Person A then left and Person C arrived. She saw person B doing something so started to do it too. And so on and so on.

Privacy

Yours

Your guests need their privacy but so do you. It's your home and by allowing strangers into it you could lose your own space. I am lucky enough to have a log cabin in my garden and it is my work room, study and chill out room. When I am in it with the door open and the blinds up, I am accessible. If I put the blinds down and close the door it is a perfect keep out signal. I am sitting in it now writing this.

Obviously, you need your own bedroom too. If you don't have another space then use that.

As my guests are usually out for most of the day, sightseeing or studying, I really do have the whole house to myself. Last year I had a friend over for coffee and we had been chatting happily for over an hour. She asked how many guests I had at the time and I said "Three". She asked if they were at university that day. I replied "no, they are all upstairs in their rooms". All three were studying for their Masters and were deep in study. The house was perfectly still and quiet. She had been unaware that anyone else was in my home.

Theirs

Your guests need their privacy from you and from each other. Never go into a guest's room without first knocking and being invited. If you need to enter for cleaning or repairs always tell them first. It is simple respect.

Room Keys

None of my bedrooms have locks. Hotel rooms have locks with keys, Bed and Breakfast rooms have locks with keys. Homes don't have locks. I don't want to go down that route. You may feel differently.

Respect The Privacy Of Other Guests

I had a young Chinese girl staying with me about three years ago. She presumably did not close her bedroom door at home as her room door in my home was always open. She would be sitting in bed with her door open so that it was impossible not to see her when anyone went to the bathroom. She was not worried about it at all, but other guests were quite embarrassed. I had to ask her to keep her door shut not just to protect her privacy but to protect my other guests too. The same young girl came down to dinner wearing only a pair of pants and a crop top. Again, I had to ask her to go and put some clothes on. She was obviously taking my strap line seriously "a home away from home". Doing this job you meet all sorts.

Respecting the privacy of others is a major concern of mine and all the more so since I made what I can only describe as a dreadful mistake. Unequivocally it was my fault. It is a funny story in some ways but, oh dear............... I still go cold when I think of it. Vittoria forgave me but I wouldn't have blamed her if she hadn't.

It began innocently enough with me having a friend to stay for the night as we were working together and it was a long way for her to go home and back for work the next day.

Vittoria had gone out for the evening. Lindsey and I had a meal and a glass or three of red wine. I don't make sensible choices after red wine as, inexplicably, my head gets muddled. I had made up a room for Lindsey, clean sheets, towels etc, as I had done before. So bed time arrived and Lindsey went to bed as did I.

I heard nothing amiss during the night and got up and went down stairs for breakfast in the morning. I found Lindsey's car gone and a note from her saying she would see me at work. Slightly odd but nothing to worry about.

Then, Vittoria walked through the front door looking tired and dishevelled.

The story emerged slowly during the day from Vittoria and Lindsey. It does have a funny side if you really try hard, but I was, and still am, mortified.

The last time Lindsey stayed, she had slept in the Beach room. This time I had made up the Britain room for her as Vittoria had moved into the Beach room.

Yes, you've got it.

I forgot to tell Lindsey which room she was in and she simply went to the room she had been in before. Through a red wine haze, she didn't notice Vittoria's things in the room so simply got into Vittoria's bed and went straight to sleep. It's straight out of a farce isn't it?

Vittoria, having arrived home and done the "who's been sleeping in my bed" routine left my home and went to a friend's room in the university halls where she slept on the floor. Lindsey, having been woken by Vittoria and being very embarrassed, got up and drove her car back to our offices and spent the rest of the night trying to sleep in her car.

VAT

Tell your guests or visitors which room they are supposed to sleep in. Oh yes, second moral, don't drink red wine.

Most guests automatically respect other people's privacy but you may have to gently say something where a problem may be brewing.

Example Of My House Rules

- My home is a non-smoking household but there is a covered area in the garden where you are welcome to smoke

- Please also ensure that you respect the privacy of others in my home and keep the noise to a minimum after 11pm

- I am happy to have your friends over to visit but please let me know first

- I do not provide facilities for self-catering

- Please enjoy yourself and treat my house as a home, it is where I live and is not an impersonal hotel

Smoking

I don't smoke so had been worried that I would have to allow it in my home. Not true. It's your home, you decide. I allow smoking on my decking but not in my home. If you are a smoker you may be happy to allow it but remember to think about the next guest to stay in the room recently vacated by a heavy smoker.

> VAT
>
> Buy some simple graphic no smoking stickers and stick one in each room and another in the hall and dining room. Job done.

Bathroom Door

Odd title I know but actually this is a piece of advice that I wish I had been given early on. It is so simple but saves lots of problems.

When a guest arrives and I am showing them around I simply say that the bathroom door stays open when no one is in it. That way, everyone can see when the room is available to them without having to disturb each other by knocking.

It's so obvious but it was about a year before I worked it out. In your home with your family, it doesn't matter so much but with strangers, this simple thing saves a lot of tension.

If you have a second bathroom or a down stairs cloakroom, the guest immediately knows to go there rather than wait nervously to see if someone comes out. If you have only one bathroom then they can choose to wait or knock.

Bathroom Etiquette

This is a much more difficult area but don't let it put you off. All problems can be solved and at best headed off before a problem forms. If your guests are from other cultures it can be a minefield of offence. Tread carefully. I have learned the hard way but it still causes me problems sometimes.

One of the local language schools finds it necessary to run a session for new students on toilet etiquette.

- Waste bin

  Most British bathrooms have a waste bin in which we throw the empty centre of the toilet roll, cotton wool, used up toothpaste etc. In a family or personal bathroom, there may be used sanitary towels, used tissues etc. What is acceptable between family members is not acceptable between strangers.

  The solution is simple. Do not put a waste bin in the bathroom. Really, don't do it. Guests can take their detritus back to their own room and put it in their own lined bin.

  Many countries have water and sewage issues that we are lucky enough not to have. This results in them not placing toilet paper in the bowl and flushing away. They have a waste bin by the toilet bowl ready to accept the soiled paper. Not something we find acceptable but is very normal for them. It was this that made me remove the waste bin from my public bathrooms. It was too nasty to deal with. Without a bin, they put the paper down the toilet. You could also put up a sign if you feel it necessary.

- Feet washing

This problem has only arisen once in seven years but it was a problem that effected other guests. The background was a young male Muslim who was staying for a few days. Muslims are required to wash their feet before praying. I have had many Muslims over the years and they have always dealt with this without causing a problem for others. However, this young man was unhappy at being in England and did not feel it necessary to take into account other people's needs. There were several issues with him, but the feet washing was the strangest.

It transpired that he sat on the edge of the bath with his feet on the floor. He then used the shower head to wash his feet. The bathroom floor is luckily tiled but the resultant swimming pool overflowed onto the landing soaking the carpet.

One of the other guests came and got me and I cleared up the mess which the young man seemed oblivious to.

- Flushing

This is a basic hygiene issue and not a cultural one. For me, it is over-kill to have a sign in the bathroom saying "don't forget to flush" most people do anyway and may be insulted. Besides which, it is not very homely unless you have toddlers.

On the few occasions that it has happened, I put a sign up for a couple of days. Then remove it. You don't need to be accusatory. The point gets made without anyone being publically embarrassed.

I did have a young Chinese girl who came from a wealthy family and had an "entitled" attitude. She did absolutely nothing to clear up after herself and was shocked at the suggestion that she should. When all else fails, you have to give up and I asked her to leave. It is your home; you do not need to put up with what can only be called anti-social behaviour.

- Cleaning the bath

  Again, most people do this automatically. If the bath is always clean, people keep it clean. If, however, your own cleaning regime falls behind it automatically gives guests permission not to follow through.

  Engender a regime of respecting others. Keep the bathroom clean and check often. Do not follow a guest into the bathroom with cleaning equipment. It will unnerve them.

- Personal items

  This was something I learned within the first few days of having guests. If you have toothpaste, shampoo, shower gel or worse still your hairbrush sitting in the bathroom, somebody will use it.

  This applies to guests who leave their things in the bathroom. Someone will cross the line and use it.

  If you have your own en-suite then your stuff is safe but it still leaves the guest items.

  Strip out everything that you don't want to be used. This gives a message that says don't leave your things in here. I do two other things. I very rarely have the problem now.

  1. On the information sheet, ask guests to keep personal items in their room.

  2. When I find things in the bathroom, I remove them and leave them outside the guest's room, if I can identify the guest. If not, I leave it on the floor outside the bathroom door.

- Toilet paper

  Guests should always have access to a spare roll in case it runs out. I keep mine in a cupboard on the wall. You can leave it there or on one of those holders. Make sure you never run out.

  When you do your house run-through with your guest, make sure that they know where the spare rolls are kept.

- Dirty underwear

  Very very rarely happens, but has been known. You cannot really stop it as it is always accidental (except for the Chinese prima donna.).

  Pick it up with a carrier bag and leave it outside the guest's bedroom door. I never mention it to save embarrassment.

- Hot water

  A shower uses less hot water than a bath and is generally quicker. In a home with multiple guests, these facts take on a greater importance. Hot water will be limited if you have a traditional water tank. More modern boilers, combi, offer constant hot water but the length of time using a bathroom may still be a problem especially if you do not also have a second toilet.

  Consider having a shower only policy.

Visitors

If you have long term guests they will make friends locally. Your home will be their home for a period of time and having friends to visit is very natural. Parties are a whole other matter of course; as are overnight guests. It's your home, your decision.

I have sometimes had guests from Europe who have had family members come to visit. Five years ago a really lovely Spanish girl stayed with me for a year on the Erasmus programme. Each term, a family member came for a weekend to visit her. Her boyfriend came three times too. It helped them to see where their daughter/sister/niece/girlfriend was staying and meet us all. It helped her with homesickness. I am still in touch with them on Facebook and she came to visit on holiday a year ago.

Make your thoughts clear in the house rules. Here is my entry:

"I am happy to have your friends over to visit but please let me know first."

Eating in the Guest Rooms

This is something that I really don't have a problem with so I don't mention it to my guests at all. As I give guests a meal in my dining room every night they don't tend to need takeaways. I also don't allow self-catering so generally hot smelly food pervading the upstairs of my home is not an issue.

If you want to ban food in your rooms add it to your house rules and put it on the information sheet in the guest rooms.

Problem Guests

You will occasionally get a guest who is a problem in some way at some point. Extra demanding, rude, takes advantage of you or is inconsiderate of others.

If all attempts to rectify through talk or demonstration fail, you may have to call it a day. Remember, your house your rules!

Sometimes you may have to remind a guest that you are not a servant. It is your home not a hotel and they are a guest and you are there to help and guide them.

If the problem guest has come from a school or agency then you should approach them for help.

Sometime young people of all nationalities make poor judgements and when they are without parental influence in a foreign country make even worse ones.

Sixteen year olds from wealthy families can sometimes display an arrogance that is unsettling. I agreed to host one such from a language school. He had a disdain for women and informed me that everything was stupid. He had a car at home and helped himself to my car keys quite openly. I reclaimed them and was therefore, in his view, also stupid. I would love to make this into a funny story but it wasn't. After three days and several other unpleasant incidents I contacted the school and he was removed.

VAT

You don't have to put up with behaviour that you find unacceptable.

Asking a guest to leave can be traumatic and unpleasant but sometimes it is your only option in order to maintain a pleasant home for your other guests and your family. Your house, your rules!

Supervision

Most of your guests will probably be adults and will not require supervision. However, if you are with a school or agency, you may be allocated a young person. They will have rules that the guest's parents will have imposed and you will be expected to follow these.

In most cases it is common sense. Allowing a sixteen year old to go to an all-night party is asking for trouble. You will need to monitor and control young people as it will be part of your contract.

The language school sent me two twelve year-old Russian girls one winter. They were really afraid initially and on the first day fell asleep huddled together on my sofa. One had her thumb in her mouth. My heart went out to them both. They were nervous of everything and tentatively trying every single thing on their plate before eating with gusto. I have no idea what they thought about English food before they arrived.

They arrived in late January and we had quite heavy snow for Southampton in early February. People were complaining, roads were closed and it was all over the news.

The girls just laughed and laughed. They thought it was very funny. They had brought their winter coats and boots and were snug and warm, while I was freezing and wet. They have many months of snow every year that is several feet deep. Shops, schools and businesses don't close, people go to work and life goes on.

Alternatively, I recently had a girl who was permanently cold, even in our summer. Temperatures in the late 20's and she was shivering and wearing a fleece. Putting the heating on was not the answer as others were hot.

VAT

We are lucky with the climate in which we live. Your guests may have a very different view of our weather.

The language schools usually want youngsters to catch buses and it is up to the host to teach them. The first day is usually fine as they are paying attention to everything around them. Subsequent days they gain confidence and can make mistakes. That is when I usually get the phone calls saying they are lost.

I always program my phone number into their phones when they arrive and give them an emergency contact card. These days I almost never get a child without a phone.

One poor lad realised he had missed his stop as soon as the bus moved off but instead of getting off at the next stop and walking back he became frightened and stayed on the bus. It went to the next town before terminating. He was now about twelve miles away, forty-five minutes late and crying. The bus driver called and we got him home no harm done.

VAT

Just because they have got it right once doesn't mean they always will.

Call To Action

- Consider what house rules you want to enforce

- Determine the method you will use to tell your guests of your rules

- Decide your policy on smoking in your home

- Remove the waste bin from the bathroom

- Depersonalise the bathroom

CHAPTER 14

LANGUAGE SKILLS

Be assured, you don't need any language skills. Not altogether true of course. You do need to be able to speak English.

I guess if you don't speak English and only advertise your rooms to guests of the language that you do speak you would manage. Your business won't be very successful as it will be very limited but it is certainly up to you.

Most foreign guests want to improve their English and understand our culture.

    a. They are usually young and nervous

    b. They could be from any one of the hundreds of other countries

    c. Length of stay varies. I have had an Italian student who came for her first year at university and stayed for five years

    d. Longer stays help your guests to build relationships with each other as well as with you

Communication Problems

Of course, language can cause some issues but they are minor and I find patience and laughter solves most problems.

I have found just as many problems with British regional accents different from my own as those with a foreign accent.

In my house, I insist on an English only rule. I enforce it with a great deal of laughter but I do enforce it. My guests respond really well to it and I have found they follow it even when I am not around.

I explain that they are in Britain to experience British culture and language and to practice.

It is tempting at first to speak to foreign students in shortened or broken English. I strongly advise against this. Remember you are not speaking to idiots. Don't ever be condescending. Believe me, they will know. But even if they don't realise you are doing it, they will pick up and emulate your speech patterns.

I have also learned to slow down my speech. I only really realised that I was doing it when my son arrived whilst we were eating one day. I suggested he made a cup of tea and I would be with him soon. When I turned back to my guests there was some amusement as they hadn't understood much of what I said to my son because I naturally sped up my speech. It stimulated conversation and was all very good natured.

Occasionally I resort to Google translate. It is an app on the first page of my phone and is quite useful for specific words. It is often used for vegetable names! Generally, I don't like translation tools. They are really good for some individual words but don't translate concepts, ideas or idioms very well. The phrase "out of sight out of mind" translating to "invisible idiots" is a well-known example.

Correcting English

This one is tricky. If you keep correcting others English they will get fed up and start to resent you and, after all, what right do you have to say someone else is wrong. However, the truth is, if the guest is in Britain to improve their English then they really like it if you help them. I usually wait a day or two and then, when an opportunity arises, I correct it and then ask if they want this help. Almost always they say yes, but don't take it for granted.

I readily admit when I don't know something or when I know it is correct but don't know the grammatical reason. It took me years to understand why "you're teasing me" is correct but "you're joking me" is not. (Intransitive and transitive verbs, look it up!)

You don't have to be an expert, just be reasonably confident with the language. If you don't want to do it, don't.

Offer Lessons

My English language skills are reasonably good and I am very happy to help and give advice, however, I am not an English teacher. I come from a family of four English teachers and wouldn't dare claim the honour.

Therefore, I do not offer paid lessons. If you have English qualifications such as TEFL or ESOL then offering lessons is a very good extra income stream.

English Only House Rule

I laugh about this with students a lot. Usually, my guests are all from different countries so English is naturally the common language. Sometimes I have couples, friends or two individual from the same country. Laughing, I say that I have an English only rule in the house. Just mentioning it, sets the expectation. Currently, I have a Chinese married couple and they always speak English to each other when they are out of their room.

For me, this is important so that other guests don't feel excluded and wonder if they are being spoken about.

Practicing English is really important for most of my guests. They usually start off quiet and shy but it quickly moves on as they gain confidence in a safe, non-judgemental environment. They also learn from each other and it emphasises the usefulness of English in a multi-lingual world.

Call to Action

- Assess your English language skills

- Consider having an English only house rule

CHAPTER 15

GROWING YOUR BUSINESS

Your business model is the description of the way you run your business successfully and the methods that you use to make money. There are lots of nice, fancy business words like:

- Customer base

- Projected revenue

- Financing

- Business strategy

- Trading practices

- Policies

- Revenue streams

- Operational processes

For most homestay hosts it is as simple as 'this is the way I run my homestay, this is how I get my guests and this is the type of guest I expect'. Don't over complicate things.

In the previous chapters we have looked at getting started and the first few guests. Now we will look at the next phase, if there is one. Many hosts are quite happy carrying on in the same way, maybe just a small tweak here and there. There is absolutely nothing wrong with that. It is the "if it ain't broke don't fix it" school of thought.

Others may want to grow their business by adding in new ideas. The first year or so can be considered 'suck it and see' but now you may want to expand. Don't be afraid to grow your business model.

With any business there are really only five ways to earn extra:

- Cut costs

- Raise prices

- Expand product range

- Increase customer base

- Diversify

Cutting Costs

When you have a full year of accounts you will be able to analyze your expenses clearly and note from where the bulk of your expenses have come.

Examine the amount you are paying to advertise and make adjustments as necessary.

I had my own website and was paying about £240 a year. Initially, I thought this was a good idea as the third party sites were charging me 15% on every booking. I thought it would save me a lot of money. However, I realised that in the previous year I had only had two bookings from my own site. I had actually paid out more than twice the money that I had earned from the two guests. I cancelled the web site.

Examine each other type of expense; you may be surprised at how much you are spending.

Raise Prices

When you initially set your rates it would have been based upon your expectations and the need to get guests. After a year of trading, you will know considerably more and will be able to make a more educated decision. I put my prices up by a small amount every year now, but for the first 2 years, the price increased by a larger amount as I learnt what the local market would support.

Expand Product Range

Adding value

Adding value to your homestay will increase your guest satisfaction and they will be more likely to give you good reviews online and recommend others to stay with you.

Value added can be very small simple things that you give away or larger things that you offer to your guests for payment.

- Umbrellas. This is Britain. It rains. Foreign guests often don't realise the rain is as frequent as it is. Keeping a supply available for your guests to use will be a welcome addition but cheap and easy to provide.

- Local information leaflets. Collect leaflets from local attractions and make them available to your guests. Some local or county councils have websites where they publish up-coming events. Print off a monthly events sheet.

- List local taxi firms or Uber so that your guests will know who to call when they are out and about.

- Bus timetables are really useful too.

- Ebook. I often get asked for some of my recipes. Write an eBook and give it away on your website or directly to your guests. If an eBook is too much, write a simple booklet and photocopy it for your guests.

Packed lunches

Tourists, students and business people often need to get their own lunch and it can be difficult depending on the location. A packed lunch for one person is a bit of a pain and having everything available may not be easy. However, packed lunches for multiple people or for multiple days may be worth doing. I provide a five piece lunch for £3.00 and thus undercut the supermarket meal deals. If you buy multi packs of crisps, water, fruit and biscuits it can give a profit of £1.00-£2.00. Not a lot in itself but after a few it adds up.

Souvenirs

Foreign guests are always looking for gifts to take back home for their family or friends. If you have a display cabinet you could put a few items in it for sale. Get creative. If you are crafty, make some things. Key rings always go down well.

Bicycle to hire

Foreign guests rarely have cars so offering them the use of a bicycle might be very welcome. If you live in the country side, bikes may also be useful. Charge a small daily rate and you will probably have many takers.

Language lessons

If you have a teaching qualification you may feel able to offer English language lessons to foreign guests. You can advertise this before a guest books or using a flyer in your home.

If you don't have the relevant qualifications you could look at doing an online TEFL course.

It may be that you know someone who would like to offer this service and would be happy to give you a small percentage as an introduction fee.

Transportation

In most cases, you are not a chauffeur. Guests are responsible for getting themselves to and from school, work and outside activities. You may want to offer a private taxi service for your guests with trips to and from airports, coach stations, out to tourist attractions or out of town shopping centres. However, there are insurance implications so check out your insurance providers. You can, of course, give your guests a lift and ask them to help with the fuel costs.

Hobbies

What do you know about that a guest would be interested in knowing? Do you like to share your skills with others? If you are an artist, maybe others would like to share your hobby.

Maybe you could offer to arrange golfing or fishing trips.

If you are knowledgeable about your local area you could offer guided tours.

Increase Your Customer Base

Increasing your customer base is about getting repeat business and gaining entirely new customers.

Repeat business

Most of your initial business will have come from schools or websites but you will begin to get previous guests contacting you to visit again or they will pass your details on to others. This is a reactive process. You wait for repeat business and recommendations. You could become proactive by sending out postcards or emails to previous customers offering discounts or just friendly updates.

Sending previous customers a Christmas card is a friendly gesture which will remind them of your existence and how nice their stay had been. Not really an option if your guests were from other countries but still worth thinking about.

Updating your Facebook page will also keep your name in front of people. Make sure you send out friend requests to previous guests or better still, while they are current guests.

New customers

Guests who come through a third party website will be asked to post a review of their stay with you a couple of days after leaving. Potential guests use these reviews to decide whether they want to stay or not. Don't underestimate their power.

If you feel that the advertising medium you are using is not giving you enough new customers, consider not using it anymore and investigate further opportunities. You can, of course, use many different sources at the same time. However, be careful to synchronise all the different diaries or you could find yourself in a mess with double bookings.

Increase conversion rate

If a potential guest makes an enquiry and then goes ahead and makes a booking they have converted from potential to guest.

Consider how many enquiries you have received that have not converted. Why? Spend a short time thinking about why and if you could do something different that would have secured the booking.

Diversify

Diversification is about changing your business model to include extra income streams. You have a successful homestay business but would like a different way of earning money in addition to the homestay.

The ultimate business expansion would be to add rooms to your home, or indeed, buy a bigger home. This would be a major undertaking. There are some simpler ways of earning a little extra.

Rent out your drive

If you have a house with off street parking you may want to consider allowing others to park their car on your drive while they are away on holiday, at an event or on business. I found this opportunity from a magazine article a few years ago. There are several sites that allow you to advertise such as Just Park or Your Parking Space.

You won't make a fortune but it all adds up.

Become an Uber driver

This is a relatively new idea. You can drive with Uber if you fulfil their requirements. You must:

- Have a valid driving licence

- Be over twenty-one

- Have a four door car registered since 2008

- Have at least one year's driving experience

- Local authority private hire licence

Uber help you get the private hire licence and can even make arrangements for a car. You work the hours that you want to work so can fit it around a homestay business easily.

Set up an ironing or laundry service

Personally, I hate ironing but luckily not everyone else does. You can earn around £10 an hour and offering a pick up drop off service will ensure that you have plenty of takers. Advertise locally, in shop windows, notice boards and supermarkets.

Become a mystery shopper.

This is quite a fun way of earning a little money. Mostly you get free meals or shopping in return for writing a review

Companies use mystery shoppers to test customer service in supermarkets, shops, pub chains, hotels and restaurants. I have stayed in four star hotels, eaten in restaurants and bought pillows from a store. Try Market Force, Mystery Shoppers and Grassroots Mystery Shopping.

Call to Action

- Decide whether to expand your business initially, wait for a year or so, or if you are happy with the status quo

- Consider ways of cutting your expenses

- Determine if raising prices is viable

- Look for ways to increase your customer base

- Decide if there are other services you can offer that will raise extra income

- Are there any ways to increase your revenue by diversification

Final Words

I hope you have enjoyed this book and that it has inspired you to take the first steps towards becoming a homestay host.

We are all in charge of our own destiny. The future is yours, now go and take it.

APPENDIX 1

WEBSITES

Visit Britain
https://www.visitbritain.org/pink-book
https://www.visitbritain.org/pink-book/fire-risk-assessment-tool

Inland Revenue
www.inlandrevenue.gov.uk

Tv Licensing
www.tvlicensing.co.uk

PRS for Music Customer Service Centre
http://www.prsformusic.com/Pages/default.aspx

Motion Picture Licensing Company (MPLC)
http://www.themplc.co.uk/files/mplctariffhotel.pdf

Information Commissioner's Office (ICO)
https://ico.org.uk/

Government Publications
https://www.gov.uk/government/publications/letting-rooms-in-your-home-a-guide-for-resident-landlords/letting-rooms-in-your-home-a-guide-for-resident-landlords

Fire Risk Assessment Template
https://www.gov.uk/government/publications/do-you-have-paying-guests

Citizens Advice
https://www.citizensadvice.org.uk/housing/renting-a-home/subletting-and-lodging/lodging/lodging/

DBS online application
https://crb-online.org.uk

Lewis School of English
http://lewis-school.co.uk/

Yvonne Halling – Bed and Breakfast Magic
https://www.bedandbreakfastcoach.com

Just Park
https://www.justpark.com/

Your Parking Space
https://www.yourparkingspace.co.uk/

Homestay.co.uk
https://www.homestay.com/united-kingdom

My own entry on Homestay.com
https://www.homestay.com/united-kingdom/southampton/20456-homestay-in-woodmill-southampton

My own entry on Facebook
https://www.facebook.com/southamptonhomestay/

Airbnb
https://www.airbnb.co.uk/

Quality Linens of Southampton
https://m.facebook.com/quality-linens-of-southampton-3626595
51176543/

Appendix 2

INFORMATION SHEET

Information Sheet

Welcome to my home. Please call me **Annette**. Here is some of the information that will help you during your stay. This is a home not a hotel, please be kind and considerate to each other.

Emergency Card	Please keep your card with you at all times. It will help you to get assiastance if necessary.
English Only	I would suggest that you impose an English only rule on yourself while in the public areas of my home. This will help you to practice and means that other guests will not feel uncomfortable.
WiFi	☐ Password ☐
My cat	Her name is Precious. She is very friendly and will allow you to pet and stroke her.
Shoes	Please remove your shoes in the house. There is a shoe store by the front door.
Washing	Put it in the basket, and when you are ready, ask how to use the washing machine. The iron and ironing board are downstairs in the tall cupboard. There are two driers to use outside to the right, for drying on the decking or inside at night. Please only use the tumble dryer in exceptional circumstances as it is expensive.
Food	If there is any food you don't like, please tell me!
Breakfast	Help yourself at any time. It will be laid out on the dining table until around 10 but you can get it from the cupboards later if I have cleared away.
Lunch	I am happy to make up a 5 piece packed lunch for you at a cost of £3.00. Sandwich, bottle of water, piece of fruit, chocolate biscuit and packet of crisps. Please let me know the night before.
Dinner	I offer FREE dinner at about 19:00 (7pm). The purpose of this is to converse together around a family table. If there is a special occassion or problem, I can plate food for you to warm up later. If you don't want to eat on any night, it would be helpful to tell me before 17:00 (5pm) so that it is not wasted. The meal is FREE so I do not offer an alternative at lunch time.
Cooking	My home is not set up for you to cook or prepare your own food. You may store personal food in the bottom drawer of the refridgerator.
Drinks/cake/fruit	Help yourself anytime.
Room Cleaning	Room will be swept, tidied, bins emptied and sheets and towels changed on a Tuesday morning. Please leave the room between 10:00 and 12:00 to allow the cleaner free access.
Bedroom	Please think about the other people in the house and also the neighbours. Please don't make a noise or take a shower after 23:00(11pm). Please be considerate of others in the house at all times. If you take plates or cups to your room, please return them to the kitchen when you have finished.
Bathroom	When you have a shower, pull the blind down first. People outside can see you if the light is on.
	Leave the door open when you have finished. This allows everyone to see that the bathroom is available.
	Please keep your personal items in your room and leave the bathroom clean ready for someone else to use.
	Please only put paper down the toilet. Everything else should be returned to your room and placed in the waste bin.
Front Door	When you leave the house at any time, please lock the front door unless you are certain that I am in the house. If you don't lift up the handle first, the door will not lock.
Fees	Please pay in full on arrival unless we have made alternate arrangements. Monthly payments are due on the first of the month. If you have booked for a specific period the full amount is due even if you leave early as the room has been made unavailable to others.
Key box	If you lose your key or leave it at home, there is a key in the box on the wall by the front door. The code is ☐ Please return it after use so someone else will have access to it.
Key	Please return your key when you leave. They cost a lot to replace. Thanks.

143

Appendix 3

EMERGENCY CARD

Annette Scott
Southampton Homestay

xxxxxx
Woodmill
Southampton
SO18 2JN

+44 (0) xxxxxxxx 51

A xxxxxxxx t@msn.com

https://www.facebook.com/
southamptonhomestay/

https://www.homestay.com/
united-kingdom/Southampton/
20456-homestay-in-woodmill-southampton

Emergency Police, Fire or Ambulance Call **999**

Local Doctor: Burgess Road Surgery, Southampton.
Call **02380 676 233**

Lewis School of English, 33 Palmerston Road, Southampton.
Call Michelle Sandford **02380 228 230**

APPENDIX 4

EVACUATION PROCEDURE

Fire Evacuation

In the case of a fire exit down the stairs and out of the front door

If the stairs are blocked, exit via the window onto the roof and into the rear garden

Emergency number for Fire, Ambulance and Police

999

APPENDIX 5

MENU PLAN

Week 1	Main	Vegetarian	Protein	Carb	Vegetable	Pudding
Sunday	Roast Pork	Stuffed Pepper	Pork	Roast	Sweetcorn / Sprouts	Yoghurt
Monday	Garlic Chicken	Veg Burger	Chicken	Chips	Sweetcorn / Carrots	Ice Cream
Tuesday	Cheese & Pot Pie and Gammon	Cheese & Pot Pie and Veg Burger	Gammon	Mash	Peas / Tomatoes	Fruit Crumble
Wednesday	Chilli Con Carne	Chillin San Carne	Beef	Rice	Salad	Jelly / Mousse
Thursday	Orange Chicken	Orange quorn	Chicken	Mash	Brocolli / Carrots	Saucy Lemon Pud
Friday	Spag bol	Spag bol quorn	Beef	Pasta	Salad	Yoghurt
Saturday	Sausage and Mash	Veg sausages	Sausages	Mash	Baked Beans	Bread & Butter Pud

Week 2	Main	Vegetarian	Protein	Carb	Vegetable	Pudding
Sunday	Normandy Pork	Normandy Quorn	Pork	Roast	Green Beans	Trifle
Monday	Beef Stew	Veg Casserole	Beef	Mash	Carrots / Green Beans	Pineapple Upside Down
Tuesday	Lamb Tagine	Cauliflower Tagine	Lamb	Rice	Salad	Ice Cream
Wednesday	Chicken Tetracini	Mushroom Tetracini	Chicken	Pasta	Salad	Yoghurt
Thursday	Cottage Pie	Veg Cottage Pie	Beef	Mash	Green Beans	Mini Pot Puddings
Friday	Fish	Veg Burgers	Fish	Chips	Peas	Ice Cream
Saturday	Roast Pork	Stuffed Aubergine	Pork	Roast	Carrots / Sprouts	Yoghurt

Week 3	Main	Vegetarian	Protein	Carb	Vegetable	Pudding
Sunday	Pasta bake	Pasta bake	Beef	Pasta	Salad	Jelly / Mousse
Monday	Grilled Fish	Veg Burgers	Fish	Vegetable Rice		Ice Cream
Tuesday	Cheese & Pot Pie and Gammon	Cheese & Pot Pie and Veg Burger	Gammon	Mash	Peas / Tomatoes	Fruit Crumble
Wednesday	Sausage Casserole	Sausage Casserole	Pork	Roast	Sweetcorn / Cabbage	Yoghurt
Thursday	Chicken Pie	Quorn Pie	Chicken	Mash	Brocolli / Carrots	Saucy Lemon Pud
Friday	Spag bol	Spag bol	Beef	Pasta	Salad	Bread & Butter Pud
Saturday	Sausage and Mash	Veg Sausages	Sausages	Mash	Baked Beans	Yoghurt

Week 4	Main	Vegetarian	Protein	Carb	Vegetable	Pudding
Sunday	Quiche	Stuffed Aubergine	Eggs	Chips	Sweetcorn	Yoghurt
Monday	Cottage Pie	Veg cottage pie	Beef	Mash	Carrots / Green Beans	Ice Cream
Tuesday	Normandy Pork	Normandy Quorn	Pork	Roast	Green Beans	Trifle
Wednesday	Chicken Supreme	Creamed Mushrooms	Chicken	Vegetable Rice		Ice Cream
Thursday	Pasta bake	Pasta Bake	Beef	Pasta	Salad	Yoghurt
Friday	Fish	Veg Burgers	Fish	Chips	Peas	Mini Pot Puddings
Saturday	Chilli Con Carne	Chillin San Carne	Beef	Rice	Baked Beans	Ice Cream

PACKED LUNCH OFFER

Packed Lunches Available

£3.00

Baguette or Bread: Egg Mayo, Ham, Tuna Mayo, Cheese

Crisps: Cheese and Onion, Ready Salted, Beef

Bottle Water

Fruit: Apple, Banana, Orange

Chocolate Biscuit

Please give me a couple of hours notice

DIARY

Day	Month	Day	Date	Event		Achieved	Sleeping				Parking		
							Britain	Beach	Butterfly	London	Bal side	Mid	Zoe side
2	January	Tuesday	2nd	sandy to airport			Vittoria		Chandler	Hamza			
3	January	Wednesday	3rd	Hamza leaves Bernard arrives		rooms changed	Vittoria		Chandler	Bernard			
4	January	Thursday	4th	larry to cruise £100 complete Mum shopping			Vittoria		Chandler	Bernard	Larry		
5	January	Friday	5th	Jan and Paul morning			Vittoria		Chandler	Bernard	Larry		
6	January	Saturday	6th			bernard to charity shop	Vittoria	Bernard	Chandler		Larry		
7	January	Sunday	7th	mum and dad		chelle to m&D then	Vittoria	Bernard	Chandler		Larry		
8	January	Monday	8th				Vittoria	Bernard	Chandler		Larry		
9	January	Tuesday	9th	mum to doctor 10.40 Pick up Dane 5.40 gatwick	chell clean	coffee in garden	Vittoria	Bernard	Chandler		Larry		
10	January	Wednesday	10th		Amy		Vittoria	Bernard	Chandler		Larry		
11	January	Thursday	11th	Dad to nightingale 11.30 blood test		in garden centre	Vittoria	Bernard	Chandler		Larry		
12	January	Friday	12th				Vittoria	Bernard	Chandler		Larry		
13	January	Saturday	13th				Vittoria	Bernard	Chandler		Larry		
14	January	Sunday	14th	mum and dad nicole and mitch		zip in verena's skirt	Vittoria	Bernard	Chandler		Larry		
15	January	Monday	15th	karen coming		penny table	Vittoria	Bernard	Chandler		Larry		
16	January	Tuesday	16th	**Mum shopping**	chell clean		Vittoria	Bernard	Chandler		Larry		
17	January	Wednesday	17th				Vittoria	Bernard	Chandler		Larry		
18	January	Thursday	18th	Emily house hunting 11	emily		Vittoria	Bernard	Chandler		Larry		

MY WWW.HOMESTAY.COM DESCRIPTION

I specialise in university students during the academic year, but am also happy to accept both Brits and others throughout the year for shorter time periods. My home provides a safe and studious environment that is nurturing where necessary, yet allows freedom with security.

BREAKFAST AND A FREE EVENING MEAL IS INCLUDED IN THE PRICE.

I can also provide a packed lunch (baguette, crisps, fruit, bottle water, choc biscuit). Available on request for £3.00

I have a large open plan down stairs which creates a pleasant social environment and a covered decking area for smokers and non-smokers alike.

We usually eat together at around 7pm where we can chat and catch up on each other's day. It is an opportunity to practice English, enjoy English cooking and emerce yourself in English day to day life. I am happy to keep food for the occasions when you need to be later.

There are beautiful walks and a running track along the river which is less than 2 mins away. The buses go from the next street and take 20 mins into the city and to the general hospital and 10mins to the main university campus.

Southampton airport is 1 mile as is the mainline station to London. The London coaches also stop at the university.

Lightning Source UK Ltd.
Milton Keynes UK
UKHW012243230219
337875UK00005B/213/P